# The
# Inquisition

# The
# Inquisition

## Don Nardo

**LUCENT BOOKS**

*An imprint of Thomson Gale, a part of The Thomson Corporation*

Detroit • New York • San Francisco • New Haven, Conn. • Waterville, Maine • London

LIBRARY OF CONGRESS CATALOGING-IN-PUBLICATION DATA

Nardo, Don, 1947-
  The Inquisition / by Don Nardo.
      p. cm. -- (World history series)
  Includes bibliographical references and index.
  ISBN-13: 978-1-59018-653-4 (hardcover)
  1. Inquisition. I. Title.
  BX1713.N37 2007
  272'.2--dc22

2007021479

ISBN-10: 1-59018-653-2
Printed in the United States of America

# Contents

# Foreword

Each year, on the first day of school, nearly every history teacher faces the task of explaining why his or her students should study history. Many reasons have been given. One is that lessons exist in the past from which contemporary society can benefit and learn. Another is that exploration of the past allows us to see the origins of our customs, ideas, and institutions. Concepts such as democracy, ethnic conflict, or even things as trivial as fashion or mores, have historical roots.

Reasons such as these impress few students, however. If anything, these explanations seem remote and dull to young minds. Yet history is anything but dull. And therein lies what is perhaps the most compelling reason for studying history: History is filled with great stories. The classic themes of literature and drama—love and sacrifice, hatred and revenge, injustice and betrayal, adversity and overcoming adversity—fill the pages of history books, feeding the imagination as well as any of the great works of fiction do.

The story of the Children's Crusade, for example, is one of the most tragic in history. In 1212 Crusader fever hit Europe. A call went out from the pope that all good Christians should journey to Jerusalem to drive out the hated Muslims and return the city to Christian control. Heeding the call, thousands of children made the journey. Parents bravely allowed many children to go, and entire communities were inspired by the faith of these small Crusaders. Unfortunately, many boarded ships captained by slave traders, who enthusiastically sold the children into slavery as soon as they arrived at their destination. Thousands died from disease, exposure, and starvation on the long march across Europe to the Mediterranean Sea. Others perished at sea.

Another story, from a modern and more familiar place, offers a soul-wrenching view of personal humiliation but also the ability to rise above it. Hatsuye Egami was one of 110,000 Japanese Americans sent to internment camps during World War II. "Since yesterday we Japanese have ceased to be human beings," he wrote in his diary. "We are numbers. We are no longer Egamis, but the number 23324. A tag with that number is on every trunk, suitcase and bag. Tags, also, on our breasts." Despite such dehumanizing treatment, most internees worked hard to control their bitterness. They created workable communities inside the camps and demonstrated again and again their loyalty as Americans.

These are but two of the many stories from history that can be found in the pages of the Lucent Books World History series. All World History titles rely on sound research and verifiable evidence, and all give students a clear sense of time, place, and chronology through maps and timelines as well as text.

All titles include a wide range of authoritative perspectives that demonstrate the complexity of historical interpretation and sharpen the reader's critical thinking skills. Formally documented quotations and annotated bibliographies enable students to locate and evaluate sources, often instantaneously via the Internet, and serve as valuable tools for further research and debate.

Finally, Lucent's World History titles present rousing good stories, featuring vivid primary source quotations drawn from unique, sometimes obscure sources such as diaries, public records, and contemporary chronicles. In this way, the voices of participants and witnesses as well as important biographers and historians bring the study of history to life. As we are caught up in the lives of others, we are reminded that we too are characters in the ongoing human saga, and we are better prepared for our own roles.

**476**
Traditional date for the fall of Rome and beginning of Europe's medieval era (or the Middle Ages).

**1431**
*The Inquisition arrests, tries, and executes the French warrior-maiden Joan of Arc.*

**1095–1099**
*Years of the First Crusade, in which European nobles and others lead armies to Palestine to "liberate" the region from Muslims.*

**ca. 1280**
The Mongol Empire, created by Genghis Khan, reaches its greatest extent.

**1478**
Spain's King Ferdinand and Queen Isabella create the Spanish Inquisition.

| 400 | 1000 | 1100 | 1200 | 1300 | 1400 |

**634**
Beginning of a series of Arab conquests of the Near East and North Africa.

**1347**
The bubonic plague (or Black Death) strikes Europe with terrifying rapidity and severity, killing millions.

**1492**
Sailing from Spain, Italian-born mariner Christopher Columbus lands in the West Indies, initiating a great age of global exploration.

**1233**
Pope Gregory IX establishes the medieval Inquisition.

**1497**
*Portuguese explorer Vasco da Gama sails eastward around Africa and reaches India.*

# Time of the Inquisition

**1542**
The Roman Inquisition is established to protect the Catholic Church from Protestantism and other so-called heresies.

**1607**
*English settlers land at Jamestown, in Virginia, the first of Britain's American colonies.*

**1966**
The Catholic Church abolishes its index of banned books, begun by the Roman Inquisition in the 16th century.

**1776**
The United States declares its independence from Britain.

| 1500 | 1600 | 1700 | 1800 | 1900 | 2000 |
|------|------|------|------|------|------|

**1543**
*Polish astronomer Nicolas Copernicus publishes his* On the Revolutions, *which advocates the heliocentric view of the universe.*

**1618–1648**
Catholics and Protestants clash in Europe's Thirty Years War, which devastates large portions of Germany.

**1600**
The Roman Inquisition burns scientist Giordano Bruno at the stake for proposing that the stars are other suns.

**1939–1941**
*Years of World War II, the single most destructive war in history. More than 50 million people die.*

# Trying to Examine the Inquisition Impartially

The modern word inquisition comes from the ancient Latin terms *inquiro,* meaning "to seek out," and *inquisition,* meaning "a search."

Today the word is rarely used to describe a search. Instead it usually refers to an infamous medieval institution known as the Inquisition. It consisted of a series of ecclesiastical, or church-sponsored, courts created to find, bring to trial, and punish or otherwise suppress heretics that the Catholic Church deemed threatening to its existence. A heretic is a person whose beliefs or actions go against the traditional beliefs and rituals of a given faith.

It should be emphasized that the term Inquisition is one that modern historians and other observers use as a matter of convenience. In reality there was no single inquisition conducted by the Church for centuries without interruption, but rather the Inquisition consisted of a series of separate, individual inquisitions that were

held in various places at various times. The first, which began in the early 1200s, is usually referred to as the medieval, or papal, Inquisition. Its original goal was to deal with heretics in France, but it eventually operated in other countries as well. Its most famous victim was the renowned French warrior-maiden, Joan of Arc. In the late 1400s, another Inquisition started in Spain. The Spanish Inquisition, which is the most famous of the inquisitions, was designed to rid Spain of non-Catholics, especially Jews and Muslims. (There were also branches of the Spanish Inquisition in Portugal and the Spanish and Portuguese colonies in North and South America.) Still another Catholic institution created to deal with heretics was the so-called Roman Inquisition, which began in the mid-1500s. This version of the Inquisition became famous for persecuting early modern scientists whose ideas appeared to go against the Bible and church doctrine. The best known victim of the Roman Inquisition was the Italian astronomer Galileo. Because all of these inquisitions had similar goals, used similar methods, and were all supported to one degree or another by the Catholic Church, it has become routine to refer to them collectively as the Inquisition.

## The Brutal Product of a Brutal Age

Today the activities and events of the Inquisition involve some distasteful, disturbing, and even frightening images. This is partly because of the intolerance shown by the inquisitors (the men in charge of searching for and trying heretics). Anyone who dared to think or worship in ways that deviated from Catholic traditions was subject to arrest and trial. These trials were not fair, impartial proceedings like those in modern democracies; instead, in an Inquisition trial the accused was presumed to be guilty from the start and forced to confess his or her guilt. Also, the tactics employed to obtain these confessions were often brutal and inhumane.

*A Spanish Jew faces the Grand Inquisitor during the Spanish Inquisition, the most famous of the inquisitions.*

Over the centuries, thousands of people underwent horrendous tortures, and many suffered agonizing deaths, often being burned alive. Indeed, the Inquisition has come to be closely associated with the concepts of intolerance, injustice, torture, and murder.

But was the Inquisition more intolerant than other medieval institutions? And were the inquisitors the only authority figures in Europe who conducted torture and grisly executions? A number of historians and other modern observers are quick to point out that they were not. According to this view, the methods and deeds of the various inquisitions should be examined and judged within the context of the ages and societies in which they took place. Although the Inquisition may be considered corrupt and brutal by today's standards, these activities were much more commonplace in their time. As scholars Michael Baigent and Richard Leigh put it:

> The Inquisition was the product of a brutal, insensitive, and ignorant world. Not surprisingly, it was itself in consequence brutal, insensitive, and ignorant. It was no more so, however, than numerous other institutions of its time. . . . Many of the . . . worst excesses were caused by individuals acting with what, according to the knowledge and morality of their time, they deemed the best and worthiest of intentions. We would be rash to imagine our own worthy intentions as being infallible.[1]

Edward Peters, of the University of Pennsylvania, a noted scholar of the Inquisition, agrees. He points out that at the time that the Inquisition began to root out heretics, the severity of criminal law and the use of torture were already commonplace in Europe's secular (non-religious) courts. "A good deal of Inquisition history," Peters says,

> has been written as if the papal inquisitors were the only ardent pursuers of alleged wrongdoers in thirteenth-century Europe. In fact, they were always less numerous, and often less ardent, than the judicial servants of secular powers.[2]

Indeed, secular authorities and courts in medieval Europe routinely used methods and punishments such as torture and burning at the stake. Moreover, the secular

*During the centuries of the Inquisition, thousands of people underwent horrendous forms of torture.*

authorities often persecuted the same groups that the Catholic inquisitors did. Jews, Muslims, and Protestants, for example, all major victims of the Inquisition, were also frequent targets of kings and their soldiers and prosecutors for political reasons or because of simple hatred. Also, the Inquisition prospered during an age in which women and children were routinely beaten by husbands and fathers; people believed in witches and thought that demons could take possession of people's bodies; and slavery was thought to be perfectly ethical and supported by God.

## The Protestants and the Black Legend

Another reason that the Inquisition's bad reputation must be examined and judged with care is that some of that reputation may not be totally deserved. Peters and another major modern scholar of the Inquisition, Henry Kamen, point out that many modern depictions of the various inquisitions exaggerate both their degree of organization and the number of victims they killed. This, the scholars say, is largely because of propaganda spread by Protestant writers from the 1500s well into the 1800s. These were the years in which Protestantism separated from Catholicism, creating much animosity on both sides, and many Protestant denominations sought to distance themselves from Catholic ideas and rituals.

Thus, perhaps not surprisingly, the goal of these Protestant writers was to discredit the Catholic Church as completely as possible. Such propaganda depicted the Inquisition as a large arm or department of the Catholic Church that existed as a monolithic unit for some seven centuries. That church department was supposedly designed to deprive non-Catholics of their liberty. As Kamen writes: "Protestant pens depicted the struggle of heretics as one for freedom from a tyrannical faith. Wherever Catholicism triumphed, they claimed, not only religious but also civil liberty was extinguished."[3]

Yet only during some periods was the Inquisition a formal, well-organized department within the Church. Often, tribunals intended to root out heretics were set up in various countries on an as-needed basis. Each was a separate, mainly local institution, unrelated to the others. Moreover, sometimes the church and its leader, the pope, had little or no direct control over the inquisitors. In the case

*As a result of the Spanish Inquisition, William of Orange claimed that the Spaniards were bloodthirsty barbarians.*

of the Spanish Inquisition, for example, most of the inquisitors worked directly for and took their orders from Spain's king and queen, sometimes to the frustration of the popes in Rome.

In another case in which the facts were later distorted, the horrors of the Spanish Inquisition were also used by the rulers of various European countries to disparage and discredit Spain. This is because these rulers and their countries often viewed Spain as their political, economic, and military enemy. The common charge was that Spaniards were an uncivilized, inferior people because they and their corrupt rulers had conducted the Spanish Inquisition. In his 1581 tract, the *Apologia*, for instance, the noted Dutch Protestant statesman William of Orange claimed that Spaniards were barbarous and bloodthirsty. He cited "the brightness of the fires" of the Inquisition, "wherein they have tormented so many poor Christians."[4]

Thus was born the so-called "Black Legend," that held that Spain was a land of fanaticism and cruelty. Typical was the claim of a Puritan preacher who wrote that when French troops invaded Spain in 1808 during the Napoleonic Wars, they found secret torture chambers that had been used by the Spanish Inquisition:

> Here they found the instruments of torture. . . . The first instrument noticed was a machine by which the victim was confined and then, beginning with the fingers, all the joints in the hands, arms, and body were broken . . . until the sufferer died. [Another device consisted of] a large doll, richly dressed and having the appearance of a beautiful woman, with her arms extended ready to embrace her victim. . . . A spring caused the diabolical engine to open [and] its arms immediately clasped him, and a thousand knives cut him into as many pieces.[5]

Such descriptions were gross distortions of the truth. No such torture devices ever existed in Europe or anywhere else.

## No Excuse for Inhumane Practices

Yet these and other myths about the Spanish Inquisition, as well as the medieval and Roman Inquisitions, must not be cited to excuse the inhumane practices of these religious tribunals. Ample evidence shows that they and their agents did perpetrate what are now viewed as despicable acts. In an attempt to enforce religious conformity, they did arrest people, confiscate their property, convict them without fair trials, torture them, and in some cases burn them at the stake or strangle them to death. Even if these practices were commonplace in medieval European society as a whole, they were still ignorant, brutal, and cruel.

Indeed, even modern Catholic authorities sometimes admit the reality of some of the Inquisition's excesses. One modern edition of the Catholic Encyclopedia for School and Home said of the Inquisition:

> Historical evidence forces us to admit that on occasion inquisitors . . . committed grave crimes against justice, charity, and the human person by summarily condemning large numbers of heretics to death. The Inquisition not only offends modern ideals of justice and spiritual freedom, it also contradicts the teaching of the Fathers and Doctors of the Church, such as St. Bernard, who said: "Faith must be the result of conviction and should not be imposed by force."[6]

Still, the vast majority of scholars and other modern observers of the Inquisition agree that the object of studying it today should not be to pass judgment on the inquisitors. All decent, reasonable people can agree at the outset that a good many of the methods the Inquisition used are uncivilized by modern standards. It is far more important, the experts say, to examine how the Inquisition came into being and what fueled its various manifestations over the centuries. It is also important to look at the victims of the Inquisition. How did their persecution, and in some cases their near or complete elimination from certain countries, affect the histories of those nations? Sometimes the Inquisition's victims were not people, but ideas. This was the case when inquisitors went after Galileo and other thinkers who claimed that the sun, not Earth, lay at the center of the universe. What effects did these attempts to halt scientific progress have on science, society, and the Church itself?

In short, the ignorance and intolerance of the inquisitors and the terrible suffering they caused cannot be erased by condemning and dismissing them. In contrast, by trying to understand them and their motives, people today can better understand themselves and their own roots. An impartial examination of the Inquisition reveals some of the ways that, for good or ill, both religious faith and religious intolerance have helped to shape the modern world.

*Although conducted by the Catholic Church, the Inquisition was also condemned by many Doctors of the Church, such as St. Bernard.*

# Chapter One

# The Medieval Inquisition: Origins and Methods

The first Inquisition is usually called the medieval, or papal, Inquisition. It came into being in the 13th century because the leaders of the Roman Catholic Church felt threatened by various groups of people across Europe who had expressed religious ideas and views that questioned or contradicted those of the Church. In the eyes of church leaders, this made them heretics.

The members of the first group to challenge established Christian beliefs in a major way were the Cathars, who lived mainly in southern France. The Cathars took their name from the Greek word *katharoi* (kuh-THAR-ee), meaning "pure." They felt that the best way to show devotion to God was to renounce all luxury and to adopt the same kind of spare lifestyle that the Bible said Jesus and his Apostles had. The Cathars also questioned a number of widely accepted

Christian beliefs; they did not think that Jesus was divine, for example.

Pope Innocent III (reigned 1198–1216), one of the strongest popes of the medieval period, was alarmed by what he saw as the heresy of the Cathars. He called them the "little foxes that spoil the vines."[7] In Innocent's view, the "vines," consisting of Christian European society and the Catholic Church, had to be protected from the foxes. So he went after the Cathars, and his efforts to rid Europe of their heresy created the beginnings of the medieval Inquisition. Later popes then built on these foundations while continuing to persecute the Cathars and trying to root out other perceived heretics as well.

*Opposite: This illumination shows the capture of Montségur castle in France where Pope Innocent III ordered 200 Cathars burned alive.*

# The Church: Society's Spiritual Guide and Protector

People living in modern democracies, where freedom of religion is taken for granted, may find this medieval preoccupation with quashing heretics a bit odd. Why did the popes and other medieval Catholic leaders feel so threatened simply because a few people wanted to worship in a different way? To understand why these churchmen felt threatened and why the Inquisition was created, one must first appreciate the crucial and often overpowering role the Church played in medieval society.

Indeed, the Roman Catholic Church, which had developed during the last two centuries of the Roman Empire, became Europe's most powerful and influential institution after Rome fell in the late 5th century. In the centuries that followed, virtually every European who was not already a Christian became one, and people came to see the Church as a major guiding force in their lives. The clergy, from the popes in Rome to local bishops and parish priests, dictated what behavior was moral and acceptable, based on the Bible and various rulings by the popes. "All over Europe there was one church only," noted scholar Anne Fremantle writes.

> If a man were not baptized into it, he was not a member of society. Anyone excommunicated [expelled from the Church and thereby denied salvation] . . . lost his political and legal rights as well. . . . It was the Church that insisted that the poor did not have to fast as much as the rich, and which forbade servile work on Sunday. It was the Church which provided the poor with social services—free food and hospitalization. There was, for a long while, no other source of education.[8]

The popes and other church leaders came to see it as both their duty and their right to maintain such tight control of people's lives. They believed wholeheartedly that their God was the only one that existed and that their religion was the only legitimate one. All other gods and faiths were false, and the members of the Christian flock had to be protected from errant religious beliefs and practices so that they would not be condemned to spend eternity in hell. Any deviation from established beliefs and rituals seemed to undermine the Church's authority. This simply could not be tolerated. On the one hand, like authority figures in all places and times, medieval churchmen were extremely reluctant to give up extensive powers to which they felt they were entitled. On the other hand, they sincerely believed that any erosion of church authority would be bad for society and go against God's will.

As a result church leaders reasoned it was necessary to maintain the blind devotion of all Christians. Most popes strove toward the goal of theocracy, a system in which the Church would have supreme authority over secular as well as ecclesiastical affairs. However the

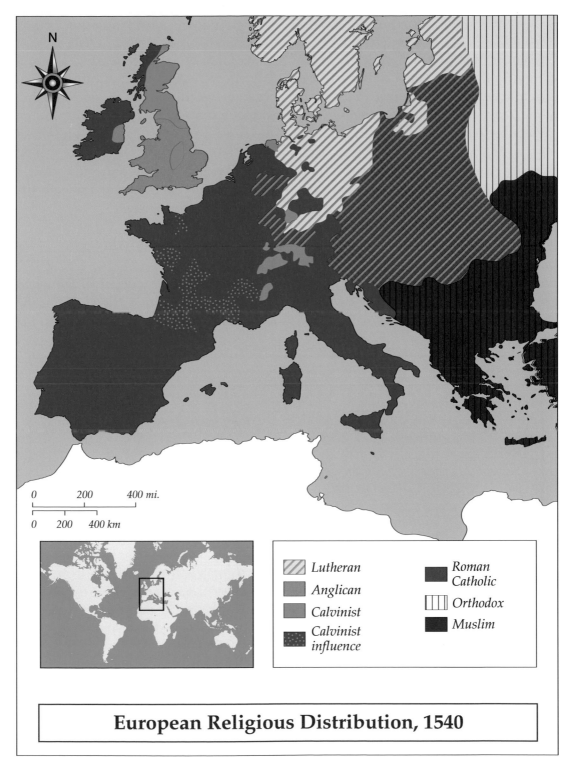

N

| 0 | 200 | 400 mi. |
| 0 | 200 | 400 km |

## European Religious Distribution, 1540

kings and nobles, though themselves devout Christians, were often reluctant to hand over their power completely to the clergy. So there ensued a centuries-long struggle between the popes and secular leaders over whose powers should be greater. In the meantime the Church was a great deal more successful in controlling the masses of ordinary Christians throughout Europe. One way that such control was maintained was through fear. In sermons, in written documents, and even in art, clergymen made it clear that people who did not adhere strictly to the traditional articles of the faith would be damned to hell. "Hell's torments were lovingly dwelt on and elaborated", scholar Louise Collins points out. "Every kind of roasting, screwing [twisting metal screws into the flesh], beating, boiling, disemboweling [cutting out the internal organs], was described in words, paint, and sculpture."[9] Disagreeing with church doctrines was seen not just as an honest difference of opinion, therefore; rather, it was labeled heresy and viewed as a serious crime that threatened society, the Church, and God himself.

## The Attractions of Catharism

Thus, when Pope Innocent III launched his campaign against the Cathars, he truly believed that he was acting in the

# A Contemporary Description of the Cathars

*Bernard Gui, one of the inquisitors sent by the Catholic Church to France to root out heretics, described the Cathars this way:*

In the first place, they usually say of themselves that they are good Christians who do not swear, or lie, or speak evil of others; that they do not kill any man or animal, nor any thing having the breath of life, and that they hold [firm to] the faith of the Lord Jesus Christ. . . . They moreover talk to the laity [rank and file Christians] of the evil lives of . . . prelates [high-placed clergymen] of the Roman Catholic Church. . . . Then they attack and vituperate [abuse], one after the other, all the sacraments of the Church, especially the sacrament of the Eucharist [or Holy Communion], saying that it cannot contain the body of Christ. . . . Of Baptism, they assert that water is material and corruptible, and is therefore the creation of the Evil Power [Satan] and cannot sanctify the soul.

Quoted in Leon Bernard and Theodore B. Hodges, eds., *Readings in European History*. New York: Macmillan, 1958, pp. 141–142.

interest of God and the people making up his flock. The pope felt it was his solemn duty to maintain the integrity of God's established church and to save souls, including those of the Cathars themselves. Surely, he reasoned, it was heresy to advocate, as the Cathars did, that Jesus was not divine; that the Church, its clergy, and its sacred sacraments (including marriage) were illegitimate and unneeded; that there was no such place as hell; and that after death some people were reincarnated as animals. By believing such things, Innocent felt, the Cathars were damning themselves in God's eyes. In addition, they were dangerous because they were constantly convincing traditional Catholics to join their heretical faith.

Indeed, the Catharist community was rapidly growing in France. This was partly because of the seemingly virtuous manner in which most Cathars conducted themselves. They were pacifists, like today's Quakers, and they claimed that they never lied or spoke evil of anyone else. Most importantly, they regularly preached that all people should model their lives after those of Jesus and his Apostles, who had neither wealth nor an established church. Typical of a number of favorable descriptions of the Cathars from that era is this one by an anonymous observer:

The good Christians [i.e., the Cathars] have come into this land. They follow the path of Saint Peter, Saint Paul, and the other Apostles. They follow the Lord. They do not lie. They do

*Pope Innocent III felt it was his duty to launch a campaign against the Cathars, whom he considered heretics.*

not do to others what they would not have others do to them. . . . [The Cathars] are the only ones to walk in the ways of justice and truth. . . . Salvation is better achieved in the faith of these men called heretics than in any other faith.[10]

Seeing that more and more people regarded Catharism as an attractive alternative to traditional Christianity, Pope Innocent III decided that he must try to stifle the Cathars. At first he employed mostly non-violent means. For instance, he ordered the bishops who oversaw church affairs in the main areas where the Cathars lived to warn about the evils of

Catharism in their sermons. The bishops also sent parish priests to reason with and hopefully reconvert Cathars to traditional Christianity. Because of the major role played by the bishops in these endeavors, the Church's early anti-Catharist campaigns are sometimes collectively called the "Episcopal" Inquisition (after *episkopos*, the Greek word for bishop).

## "The Stick Will Prevail"

However these largely peaceful efforts to quell the Cathars were unsuccessful, and the heretical movement continued to grow. In 1208, therefore, Pope Innocent III felt he had no choice but to resort to forceful means. The subsequent military campaign against the Cathars came to be called the "Albigensian crusade," after the French town of Albi, one of the major strongholds of the Cathars. Answering the pope's call, thousands of knights, foot soldiers, and adventurers from all across Europe began to converge on southern France. Some were definitely motivated by feelings of duty to the pope and the Church. Others were convinced to join the crusade because Innocent promised that each participant would get a full pardon for any sins he had committed in

*Arnald-Amaury oversees the burning of heretics in the town of Béziers. This is where he delivered his famous remark, "Kill them all. God will recognize his own."*

# What Did It Cost to Burn Someone?

*The inquisitors who ran the medieval Inquisition almost always kept detailed records of everything they did, including all monies expended. Following is an accounting of the costs (in coins called sols and deniers) for burning four heretics on April 24, 1323 in France:*

> For large wood: 55 sols 6 deniers.
> For vine-branches: 21 sols 3 deniers.
> For straw: 2 sols 6 deniers.
> For four stakes: 10 sols 9 deniers.
> For ropes to tie the convicts: 4 sols 7 deniers.
> For the executioners, each 20 sols: 80 sols.

Quoted in Henry C. Lea, *A History of the Inquisition of the Middle Ages.* 4 vols. New York: Harbor Press, 1955, vol. 1, p. 553.

his life. Still others were drawn solely by the prospect of collecting loot, as all the property of the Cathars was to be confiscated and divided among the crusaders.

In the summer of 1209, an army of fifteen to twenty thousand Christian crusaders and camp followers swept across southern France. One of the towns they singled out for attack was Béziers because they had heard that Cathars dwelled there among ordinary Catholics. The crusaders breached the walls in the space of only a few hours. Then, just before the soldiers entered the town, one of the knights approached Arnald-Amaury, the papal representative who had accompanied the troops to act as their spiritual leader. How, the knight asked, should they distinguish the town's heretics from its devout Catholics? Arnald-Amaury's

cold-blooded answer has become one of the most infamous remarks in European history. "Kill them all," he said. "God will recognize his own."[11] The attackers then poured into Béziers and began massacring everyone; women and children were killed along with the men. Many of the victims were mutilated before they were killed, having their eyes torn out and noses sliced off. In all, an estimated fifteen to twenty thousand people were butchered; of these, only a few hundred were Cathars.

Following the slaughter at Béziers, the crusade dragged on because the Cathars were numerous and often hid from the crusaders. Pope Innocent realized that he needed to develop another weapon against the Cathars, one that could also be used against other heretics that might threaten the Church's authority. So he called on a group of monks to act as anti-heresy agents. Their job was to find and identify heretics and report them to the ecclesiastical authorities in Rome. The monks, who eventually came together into two formal orders—the Dominicans and Franciscans— made up the initial nucleus of what would soon become the medieval Inquisition.

The Dominicans formed around and were named for one of Innocent's most trusted agents, Domingo de Guzman, known better to posterity as St. Dominic. He began as one of the clergymen who accompanied the soldiers of the Albigensian crusade. Even in the early stages of the crusade, he showed a decided propensity for using forceful methods against the Cathars and other heretics. At one point he made a speech that said in part:

> I have sung words of sweetness to you [the Cathars] for many years now, preaching, imploring, weeping. But as the people of my country say, where blessing is to no avail, the stick will prevail. Now, we shall call forth against you . . . and will cause many people to die by the sword, will ruin

your towers, overthrow and destroy your walls, and reduce you all to servitude. . . . The force of the stick will prevail where sweetness and blessing have been able to accomplish nothing.[12]

## The Inquisition is Formally Established

Under Pope Innocent III's successor, Honorius III (reigned 1216–1227), Dominic's followers were officially recognized

*Pope Gregory IX called upon the rapidly growing Dominican order to expand their activities against heretics.*

GREGORIVS IX Hugolin? ex Comi:
tib? Signæ Anagni, nus, creat? die 20,
Martij ann.1227. Sedit an.14.men.
5.dies 3.Ob.22. Aug. an.1241.V.S.m.i.

as an order of monks. Although Dominic himself died in 1221, at the time there were already about twenty groups of Dominicans in France and Spain, and the next pope, Gregory IX (1227–1241), called upon the rapidly growing order to expand their activities against heretics. On April 20, 1233, Gregory issued a papal bull (decree) that told the local bishops:

> We have . . . determined to send preaching friars against the heretics of France and the adjoining provinces, and we beg, warn, and exhort you, ordering you . . . to receive them kindly, and treat them well, giving them in this . . . aid, that they may fulfill their office.[13]

The nature of that "office" began to become clear in a statement the pope issued directly to Dominicans just two days later: "[You] are empowered . . . to proceed against them [the Cathars and other heretics] . . . without appeal, calling in the aid of the secular arm [local non-church authorities] if necessary."[14] The monks were now official inquisitors and their mission or office, which steadily became a sort of institution, became known as the Inquisition. They now had the authority not only to hunt for and denounce heretics, but also to try and punish them. Among the punishments were confiscation of property, making it impossible to make wills or inherit property, and banishment for life. The next pope, Innocent IV (1243–1254) went a step further and allowed the inquisitors to turn condemned heretics over to the secular authorities for execution. (This was done because it was widely seen as wrong for a clergyman to take someone's life.) Innocent IV also officially condoned the use of torture during interrogations.

At first, there was considerable friction between the inquisitors and local bishops. The bishops often felt that they were in competition with the inquisitors and that punishing heretics should be, as it had been before, the job of the bishops rather than special commissioners sent by the pope. In 1273 this dispute was finally resolved by Pope Gregory X (1271–1276) when he ordered the inquisitors and bishops to work together and share authority in their efforts to eradicate heresy.

## Gruesome but Efficient Methods

By this time, the Inquisition had developed a fairly standard set of methods. In most cases, a group of inquisitors suddenly appeared in a town and ordered all the inhabitants to meet in the town square. The chief inquisitor delivered a speech called the "edict of faith." Essentially, he gave the citizenry a grace period of thirty or forty days, during which any and all heretics were urged to come forth and turn themselves in. If they admitted their sins, they would receive light punishment and be allowed to go free.

Otherwise, following the period of grace the inquisitors began to hunt down the "guilty." Suspected heretics were arrested and almost always tortured. Because it was widely viewed as unseemly for monks and other clergymen to shed blood, the torturers generally

avoided cutting the body. It became common, therefore, to cut off the victims' air supplies, or to stretch them on wooden racks, or to force water down their throats until they choked. Methods "of this kind would seem to have been contrived to cause maximum pain and minimum mess,"[15] Baigent and Leigh remark.

Not surprisingly these and other gruesome tortures nearly always resulted in confessions, whether or not the person was guilty of heresy. After a confession the victim often received further punishment. This might include confiscation of property or even death. However, some victims were allowed to go free if they implicated others in heresy. Similarly people who had confessed earlier, during the period of grace, often escaped torture and serious punishment by naming names. Thus relatives, friends, and neighbors frequently informed on one another in hopes of saving themselves, which spread fear and undermined relationships of trust throughout society. "The Inquisition was ultimately interested in quantity," Baigent and Leigh point out.

> It was quite prepared to be lenient with one transgressor, even if he were guilty, provided it could cull a dozen or more others, even if they were innocent. As a result of this mentality, the population as a

*Victims who did not admit their guilt (opposite) where often condemned to death, like this man being lead to death by a monk.*

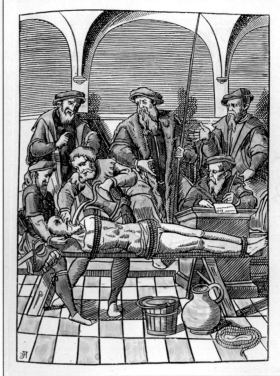

*One of the most common forms of torture used during the Inquisition was to force water down a person's throat until he or she began choking.*

> whole . . . was kept in a state of sustained dread [that made them more vulnerable] to manipulation and control. And everyone, reluctantly or not, was turned into a spy.[16]

Those victims who would not inform on others or refused to admit their own guilt were subject to the ultimate penalty. In cases in which the inquisitors handed down a death sentence, it was time for the local secular authorities to get involved. When turning victims over to civil authorities, usually town officials or

# Precedents for Brutality

The monks and others who searched out, tried, and punished heretics during the medieval and other European inquisitions were not the first legal or religious authorities to use torture in interrogations of prisoners and to burn people at the stake. In fact, the medieval inquisitors most often merely perpetuated brutal methods that European society had inherited from the late Roman Empire. For centuries torture was routinely used in Roman trials; at first it was mainly slaves who were tortured, but later free citizens suffered the same fate. Similarly, burning people alive was a common form of execution in Roman society. People who committed treason, patricide (killing one's father), arson, and sorcery were often burned at the stake. Also, during a long series of persecutions (that occurred before the Christians took charge of the Empire), Roman Christians were burned, an ironic foreshadowing of the burning of Christians by other Christians during the Inquisitions.

courts, the inquisitors recited words to this effect:

> We dismiss you from our ecclesiastical forum and abandon you to the secular arm. But we strongly beseech the secular court to mitigate its sentence in such a way as to avoid bloodshed or danger of death.[17]

This efficient system of ecclesiastical tribunals, combined with continued military crusades, eventually achieved success in the effort to suppress Catharism. In 1255 the last major Cathar fortress fell; and in the next few decades the Inquisitional courts eliminated most of the remaining Cathars. (Some surviving Cathars fled to Italy, Bosnia, and other countries, while a few remained in France and continued to practice their rituals in secret.) Despite this success the popes and their inquisitors did not feel that the threat of heresy was over. The medieval Inquisition remained in force for generations to come and in the name of God claimed many more victims.

# Chapter Two

# Victims and Martyrs of the Medieval Inquisition

The Cathars were not the only heretics identified and persecuted by the medieval Inquisition. A number of other splinter Christian groups were targeted by the Catholic inquisitors during the first two centuries or so of the Inquisition's existence. Among those the Inquisition tried to suppress were the Waldensians, who claimed the right to preach God's word without the Church's permission, and the Fraticelli, who disdained the worldliness of the clergy.

During this period the Inquisition also opposed various groups and individuals for political reasons. This was largely because many of the Church's leaders increasingly became weak, corrupt, or the tools of powerful European monarchs. One pope who refused to knuckle under to the demands of secular kings, Boniface VIII, paid a high price. In 1303, after a series of major disagreements with the strong French king Philip IV (reigned 1285–1314), Boniface excommunicated Philip. The king boldly retaliated by sending agents to kidnap the pope. Boniface was soon released. But he died only a month later and the incident sent a chill through the Church's higher offices.

As a result of pressure, from both Philip and the large number of French cardinals then in the Church's hierarchy, in 1309 Boniface's papal successor, Clement V, moved the headquarters of Roman Catholicism to the French town of Avignon. The papacy remained stationed there until 1378. Then from 1378 to 1414, two separate lines of popes, one in Avignon, the other in Rome, opposed each other. These and other events weakened the Church so much that various kings and other secular rulers were able to manipulate the Inquisition to their own political ends. The Templar Knights and Joan of Arc are the most famous victims of these political persecutions.

## The Waldensian Threat

Long before Joan was born, when the popes were still widely viewed as strong and largely independent of the influence of secular rulers, the Church still faced the threat of heretical movements. The rise of Catharism in France in the late 1100s and early 1200s demonstrated that not all Christians in Europe held exactly the same beliefs. Some followed the lead of a few charismatic dissenters. Those who established splinter groups had been born traditional Catholics, but at some time during their lives they had come to disagree with some of the Church's established ideas or rituals.

Among these dissenters was Peter Waldo, a well-to-do merchant who resided in the French town of Lyon. Around the year 1170, he underwent a major personal transformation. He decided that it was un-Christian of him to possess great wealth when there were so many poor people struggling to survive around him. So he gave away all his money and became a beggar. Waldo also became a preacher, and within a few years he had gained many followers. Numerous others among these so-called Waldensians also felt a duty and calling to preach the word of God. To make their sermons more accessible to ordinary French peasants, Waldo had a local monk translate some parts of the Bible into French. (At the time, almost all other renditions of the Bible were in Latin and could be read and studied only by a relatively few educated people, mostly clergymen and noblemen.)

The problem was that the Church had strict rules that regulated both who could preach in God's name and who could distribute copies of the Bible. Only clergymen authorized by the papal offices or local bishops were supposed to be engaged in such activities; laypersons were forbidden. Peter Waldo tried to get the Church's permission to preach

*Merchant Peter Waldo gave up all of this wealth to begin the group called the Waldensians. The Catholic Church viewed this group as a threat.*

# The Brethren of the Free Spirit

Among the many religious groups the medieval Inquisition tried to eradicate was one known as the Brethren of the Free Spirit. The Brethren first appeared in Switzerland and southern Germany in the early 1100s. Eventually, they spread into northern Germany and westward into Holland. They believed that all living things are manifestations of God, and therefore that animals, including even rats and other vermin, have souls. Because in their view a person's soul is reunited with God after death, the Brethren held that hell does not exist and that there is no need for daily, weekly, or yearly rituals like those performed in churches. The Church accused the Brethren of devil worship, an inaccurate charge, and the Inquisition went after them with a vengeance. Hundreds of the Brethren were burned or drowned before the movement was largely suppressed in the 1300s.

but was told to cease and desist. When he refused to comply, he was charged with "contempt of ecclesiastical power." Other reasons the Church opposed Waldo and his followers included some listed in a document issued by Reinerius Saccho, a papal inquisitor, in 1254:

> They despise all the statutes of the Church because they are heavy and numerous. [They also claim that] the Pope is the head of all errors . . . that the Pope and all bishops are [murderers] on account of wars [such as the Crusades] . . . that no one is greater than another in the church . . . that no one ought to bow the knee before a priest . . . that the clergy ought not to have possessions . . . that the Bishops and Abbots ought not to have royal rights; that the land, and the people, are not to be divided into parts. . . .

They also condemn all the clergy for idleness, saying that they ought to work with their hands as the Apostles did.[18]

In addition, some of the Waldensian preachers were women, something the Catholic Church would not tolerate.

The Waldensians received numerous demands from popes, bishops, and other churchmen to give up all unacceptable beliefs and practices, but most of the dissenters continued to preach and worship as they pleased. So in 1215, the Church decreed that they were heretics, and some of the crusades launched against the Cathars in the years that followed harassed or killed Waldensians as well. One problem for the inquisitors was that the Waldensians were more widely distributed than the Cathers; Waldo's followers eventually spread from France into

Germany, Spain, Italy, Austria, Poland, and elsewhere, making finding and prosecuting all of them impossible. The surviving Waldensians joined with other Protestants in their official split from Catholicism in the 1500s; some descendants of the original Waldensians still exist in Europe and the United States)

## The Church Goes After the "Little Brothers"

Another religious group that Church leaders felt must be reined in by the Inquisition was an offshoot of the Franciscan order of friars. Founded in the early 1200s by a monk named Francis of Assisi (later St. Francis), the Franciscans had been among the monks chosen by Pope Innocent III to fight the Catharist heresy. What had impressed Innocent and other church leaders about the Franciscans was their devotion to core Christian principles. The order's friars dedicated themselves to public service. They ministered to the poor and were willing to work hard day in and day out with few material rewards. In the years following Francis's death in 1226, however, many Franciscans became more worldly. Some came to live in fine houses, to wear expensive clothes, and to get involved in local political affairs. This reflected the general trend among many clergymen in recent times, especially those in high positions. Certainly the popes and bishops had come to live in luxury and to involve themselves in politics, often to the neglect of spiritual affairs.

But some Franciscans were appalled at this increasing worldliness among

*Francis of Assisi established the Franciscan order, which was at first chosen by the Catholic Church to combat heresy, but later was considered a heretical group.*

clergymen, including members of their own order. One leading friar declared in 1267: "It is a foul and profane lie to assert [the principle of] . . . absolute poverty and then refuse to submit to the lack of anything, to beg abroad like a pauper and to roll in wealth at home."[19] As a result of this attitude among some Franciscans, the order split into various factions in the late 1200s and early 1300s. Some stuck closely to the vows of poverty taken by their original founder, Francis, and refused to indulge in any sort of luxury or worldly affairs.

The popes and bishops did not like this turn of events. They worried about what the millions of laypeople they controlled would think of the extreme contrast between the poor friars and wealthy churchmen. So in 1317 they ordered the Franciscan splinter groups to join the mainstream of Franciscan and Dominican friars. One of these groups, whose members called themselves the Fraticelli, or "Little Brothers," refused. This prompted the Inquisition, by now controlled mainly by the rival Dominican order, to swing into action. The following year four of the Fraticelli were arrested, convicted of heresy, and burned at the stake.

More persecutions of the Fraticelli ensued, which distressed other Franciscans. In 1322, a group of mainstream Franciscans protested to the pope in writing and were appalled when he labeled their appeal to be heretical. The result was some two centuries of friction between the Franciscans and the Dominicans who ran the Inquisition. The inquisitors never attempted to go after the Franciscan order as a whole, but individual Fraticelli continued to be singled out for trial and punishment, and they gained a reputation as martyrs of the cause of ecclesiastical justice.

## Persecution of the Templar Knights

In the charges the Inquisition brought against the Cathars, Waldensians, and Fraticelli, some sort of religious principles had been involved. However, this was not the case with all the targets of the Inquisition's tribunals. Some were singled out for political reasons and sometimes simply out of greed for money and power. The largest of these political persecutions was that of the Templar Knights (sometimes called the Knights Templar).

The Templars were a unique combination of military and religious order. They had formed in the early 1100s, shortly after the capture of Jerusalem in Palestine, the so-called Holy Land, by Christian armies in the First Crusade. In the years that followed the Templars, who owed their allegiance to the popes, protected Christian pilgrims who journeyed to the Holy Land.

Over time, however, the Templars grew wealthy and increasingly independent of outside authority. And by 1300, they had become the single most powerful institution in Europe besides the Catholic Church itself. Baigent and Leigh sum up the bases of their power:

> The order owned immense estates across the whole of the Christian world. . . . The order owned ships, too. . . . The Templars commanded the most advanced military technology of the era. Their military resources . . . exceeded those of any other European institution. They were also the chief bankers of Europe, adept at the transfer of funds throughout Christendom. . . . And they were widely respected diplomats, able to act independently of warring factions.[20]

These impressive assets and abilities of the Templars increasingly made them the targets of jealousy and hostility by various European monarchs and even by some of the popes. In particulara King Philip IV, who had managed to make Pope Clement V his puppet in the early

*Two Templar Knights are burned at the stake. Viewed as a threat to the Church, the Templar Knights were virtually eliminated through torture and execution between 1307 and 1314.*

1300s, coveted the Templars' vast wealth; he also worried that they were planning to set up their own kingdom on French soil. In Philip's mind, the papacy and the Inquisition seemed the ideal tools to bring down the Templars, and he got Clement to issue the appropriate orders. In 1307, the Inquisition arrested all the Templars in France and seized their property. During the seven years that followed, many of the knights died either under torture or by execution. In 1314, the pope officially dissolved the Templars, although a number of them continued to live in various parts of Europe.

## The Rise of Joan of Arc

The persecution of the Templars for political reasons was not unique. In the century that followed their persecution, France once again became the scene of the Inquisition's acting in a political capacity rather than a strictly religious one. This time the victim was an individual rather than an organization. In the eyes of history, she was the single most famous person ever tried by the medieval Inquisition. Her name was Jeanne d'Arc, whom most people at the time referred to as "the Maid," or as *la Pucelle*, "the Virgin." Posterity came to call her Joan of Arc.

Joan was born in 1412 and later claimed that when she was thirteen she began to hear the voices of the long-dead Christian saints Michael, Margaret, and Catherine. Joan sincerely believed that the voices came from God and that she had been given a divine mission to fulfill. That mission was to help the French nobleman Charles VII fight the English, who at the time occupied northern France during the Hundred Years War (1337–1453).

*The most famous victim of the medieval, or papal, Inquisition was Joan of Arc.*

The young woman managed to convince Charles to allow her to lead a French army, and in 1429 she led that army to victory at Orleans and Patay. Other French successes followed. However in May 1430 Joan was captured and eventually ended up in an English prison in Rouen (in northern France).

The English feared Joan, partly because some thought she was a witch who could summon supernatural forces on the battlefield; English leaders also recognized that the Maid was a symbol of French nationalism who could still rally French armies. Simply killing Joan was not an option because she might become a martyr of the French cause. So they endeavored first to discredit her popular image as an instrument of God and make her look instead like a liar and a witch. The most effective way to do this, they reasoned, was to turn her over to the Inquisition.

## Joan's Trial and Execution

As in other trials held by the Inquisition, Joan's featured no lawyers or juries. Several noted clergymen, called assessors, acted as advisors to the judges, who were inquisitors. The assessors were allowed to ask the suspect questions, but they had no authority to pass sentence. The chief judge, Pierre Cauchon, Bishop of Beauvais, who was also the leading inquisitor and prosecutor, did most of the questioning. In fact, the first stage of the trial, which lasted more than a month, consisted of repeated sessions in which Cauchon and other judges interrogated Joan. They asked her about the miraculous voices she claimed to have heard,

for example, aiming to show that these voices had been sent by Satan.

As these sessions continued, the inquisitors did more than simply look for evidence that Joan was a heretic and witch. They also tried to discredit her in other ways, including calling into question her wearing of men's clothes (because she was a soldier). And though they repeatedly tried to get her to change into a dress, she stubbornly refused to do so. Typical was this exchange between Joan and a judge named Beaupère:

> Beaupère: Will you wear women's clothes?
>
> Joan: Give me some and I will go [leave prison a free woman]. Otherwise I will not accept them. I am satisfied with what I have on since it pleases God that I wear it.[21]

In the second phase of the trial, the inquisitors gave Joan a chance to save her soul. All she had to do, they said, was to admit her guilt and beg forgiveness from God and the Inquisition. But she refused to be intimidated and remained defiant. So Cauchon proceeded to formally charge Joan with a number of offenses against God and the Church. To make the process look legitimate, he submitted the charges to a group of outside assessors, who were asked to give their opinions in writing. These men did not rubber stamp, or automatically approve of, the charges, as he had expected they would. Instead, some of them suggested that the evidence was flimsy and that Joan might not be guilty of

# Was Saint Michael Naked?

*The inquisitors who interrogated Joan of Arc repeatedly asked her to provide details about the appearance and mannerisms of the saints that she claimed had visited her. Some of the questioning went as follows:*

**Inquisitor:** Of what form was Saint Michael when he appeared to you?

**Joan:** I saw no crown on him; and of his clothes I know nothing.

**Inquisitor:** Was he naked?

**Joan:** Do you think that God cannot afford to clothe him?

**Inquisitor:** Had he hair?

**Joan:** Why should it have been cut off? . . .

**Inquisitor:** Did Saint Michael and Saint Gabriel have natural heads?

**Joan:** Yes, so I saw them. And I believe that it was they, as certainly as I believe that God exists.

**Inquisitor:** Do you believe that God made them with heads as you saw them?

**Joan:** I saw them with my own eyes. I will not say anything else.

W.S. Scott, ed. and trans., *The Trial of Joan of Arc: Being the verbatim report of the proceedings from the Orleans Manuscript.* Westport, CT: Associated Booksellers, 1956, p. 90.

the charges. Cauchon simply ignored the assessors' opinions and proceeded with the trial, but this incident demonstrates that the medieval Inquisition was not always made up of a monolithic group of intolerant men conspiring to convict innocent people, as often depicted by detractors of the Catholic Church.

In the final stage of Joan's trial, she was once again urged to make a full confession of her guilt. When she refused, on May 24, 1431 inquisitors and guards took her to the cemetery of Rouen's Abbey of St. Ouen, where she was pronounced guilty. Then she was conveyed to Rouen's marketplace. A tall scaffold had been erected, topped by a wooden stake surrounded by bundles of wood ready to be kindled. Cauchon wasted little time in excommunicating her and turning her over to the secular authorities. One eyewitness later recalled:

She asked most fervently to be given a cross. And when an Englishman who was present heard this he made her a little one out of wood from the end of a stick, and handed it to her. She received it and kissed it most devotedly. . . . [Then] she was led off and tied to the stake [and burned]. Her last word, as she died, was a loud cry of "Jesus."[22]

Though the Inquisition managed to kill Joan, they ultimately failed to destroy her legacy. Just as English leaders had feared, she became a martyr of the French cause; moreover, the memory of her courage became a rallying cry for the French, who eventually drove the English out of France. Also, a special investigation the Church launched later found her trial to be riddled with errors and fraud and in 1456 her name was cleared. Finally, in 1920 the Catholic Church made Joan a saint. Many modern observers feel that her trial and brutal execution did more than any other incidents to permanently blacken the reputation of the medieval Inquisition.

# Second Thoughts About Killing Joan

*Years after Joan was executed, Isambart de la Pierre, an assessor at her trial, gave this testimony about the day of her death.*

One of the English, a soldier who particularly loathed Joan . . . was struck with a stupor or a kind of ecstasy when he . . . heard her crying on the name of Jesus in her last moments. He was taken to a tavern near the Vieux Marché to be restored to his senses with the aid of strong drink. And when he had eaten with a friar of the Dominican order, this Englishman confessed to the friar, who was an Englishman, that he had committed a grievous sin, and that he repented of what he had done against Joan, whom he considered a saint. For it seemed to this Englishman that he had seen a white dove flying from the direction of France at the moment when she was giving up the ghost. And the executioner . . . that same day, came to the Dominican convent and said to me that he greatly feared he was damned, for he had burned a saint.

Quoted in Wilfred T. Jewkes and Jerome B. Landfield, eds., *Joan of Arc: Fact, Legend, and Literature.* New York: Harcourt, Brace and World, 1964, p. 79.

# Chapter Three

# Origins and Goals of the Spanish Inquisition

The Spanish Inquisition is today the most famous, or perhaps more properly infamous, of the Inquisitions instituted to root out heresy in medieval and early modern Europe. The historical reputation of the Inquisition in Spain is a particularly bad one. That organization and its inquisitors have become in some ways synonymous with intolerance, injustice, torture, murder, and just plain cruelty. Modern historians have shown that in some individual instances this reputation was well deserved. In others, it has been exaggerated. Overall, the Spanish Inquisition was probably no more or less intolerant or cruel than the other European Inquisitions that came before and after it.

The Spanish Inquisition was different from other versions of the Inquisition in some crucial ways, however. First, throughout most of its existence it was not run directly by the Catholic Church and its leaders, the popes. Instead, the Inquisition in Spain was administered by the state, specifically the "Crown," meaning the royal monarchs who presided over the country. King Ferdinand (1452–1516) of the kingdom of Aragon and Queen Isabella (1451–1504) of the kingdom of Castile created the Spanish Inquisition, and later Spanish monarchs continued to sponsor it and to appoint its leading inquisitors. (Ferdinand's and Isabella's marriage in 1469 laid the foundations for the later unification of their kingdoms into the Spanish nation.)

Another important difference was that the Inquisition in Spain was used less for accomplishing religious goals, as the other Inquisitions were, and more as a means of bringing about national political and social change. In particular, it targeted certain minority groups. In the view of most Catholic Christians, who made up the majority of Spain's population, these groups were a threat to mainstream Spanish life. These minorities included Jews,

Muslims, and later various denominations of Protestants. Overall, however, average Spaniards saw Jews as the most threatening of all the country's minorities, and it was a series of attempts to drive away Jews or to convert them to Christianity that led to the creation of the Spanish Inquisition in the first place.

## Anti-Semitism in Medieval Europe

To understand the motivations behind the Spanish Inquisition, one needs to examine the widespread incidence of anti-Semitism (hatred for Jews) in Spain and other European regions in that era. Deep-seated hatred for Jews in Europe was based in part on supposed crimes they had committed in ancient times. In particular, many Christians blamed all Jews, in all ages and places, for the death of Jesus Christ. (This irrational attitude was based on the fact that the Jewish authorities in Jerusalem had helped the Romans prosecute Jesus.) Another reason that Jews came to be hated was that they clung tightly to their traditional beliefs and rituals. In a predominately Christian society in which

*Queen Isabella and King Ferdinand created the Spanish Inquisition.*

*Many Christians believed that Jews caused the spread of the bubonic plague by poisoning well water. This was one reason why Jews were persecuted during the Spanish Inquisition.*

church leaders regularly preached that Christianity was the only true religion, this made Jews seem suspect and potentially dangerous.

For these and other reasons, European Jews were often blamed for any and all ills and crimes affecting Christian communities, and various malicious myths developed that portrayed Jews as villains. One such myth claimed that Jews regularly kidnapped Christian children and butchered them in secret religious rituals. Whenever a Christian child was found dead of unknown causes, local Jews were the first suspects. Another common charge against the Jews was that they liked to steal the wafers that represent Christ's body in the Christian ceremony of Holy Communion. Supposedly, Jews pounded nails through the wafers, their sinister goal being to crucify Jesus once again.

Still another false accusation was that Jews often poisoned Christian wells and other water supplies in an effort to destroy Christian communities. The most hysterical charges of poisoning against Jews occurred during the onset of the bubonic plague (or Black Death), which spread across Europe in 1347 and 1348.

Origins and Goals of the Spanish Inquisition ■ 41

Millions of people caught the disease and died horrible deaths. Despite the fact that many of those who suffered and died were Jews, most Christians readily believed unfounded rumors that the catastrophe had been caused by Jews poisoning wells. An Italian observer wrote in April 1348:

> Some wretched [Jewish] men were found in possession of certain powders, and (whether justly or unjustly, God knows) were accused of poisoning the wells—with the result that anxious men now refuse to drink water from wells. Many were burnt for this and are being burnt daily, for it was ordered that they be punished thus.[23]

*Spanish Jews congregate in a synagogue. Before the Spanish Inquisition, Jews in Spain lived a prosperous and peaceful life.*

Indeed, whether the charge was poisoning wells, stealing wafers, or kidnapping children, Jews were regularly persecuted throughout the medieval era. It was not uncommon for angry Christian mobs to ransack Jewish communities, killing and maiming hundreds or thousands of innocent men, women, and children.

## The Jewish Communities in Spain

In spite of the rampant prejudice and sporadic violence against Jews, in some parts of Europe Jewish communities enjoyed periods of prosperity and growth. This was the case in Spain in the years immediately preceding the establishment of the Inquisition there. This prosperity, coupled with the fact that some Jews came to wield considerable social independence and financial clout, was another black mark against Spanish Jews. Joseph Perez, a noted authority on the Spanish Inquisition, explains:

> In medieval Spain, Jewish communities (known as *aljamas*) . . . enjoyed relative autonomy. . . . They administered their own affairs, under the authorities of their own magistrates. They had their own synagogues, schools, and cemeteries. . . . In this micro-society, as in [Spain's] dominant Christian society, the poor far outnumbered the rich. [But] a small minority of Jews practiced trade on a major scale and possessed fortunes which . . . enabled them to lend money to kings [and other highly placed] individuals. Sovereigns,

[bishops], and great feudal lords were happy to leave . . . the collection of taxes, tithes, and other dues [in Jewish hands]. It was this aspect of their activities that [particularly] fueled ordinary people's hatred of Jews.[24]

Thus, average Christians in Spain came to associate Spanish Jews with a multitude of perceived faults, sins, and crimes. From there it was only a small step to believing that the poverty suffered by many Spanish Christians must also be the Jews' fault. All that was needed for the government to launch a full-scale persecution, and eventually a religious inquisition, against the Jews was for a few angry people to set anti-Jewish violence in motion. As Perez puts it:

> Small groups of agitators had no difficulty in turning against the Jews the resentment of sections of the population driven to despair by a seemingly endless distress, the causes of which they could not understand. They were shocked by the opulence of a minority of Jews and became convinced that they [the Christians] were the victims of an injustice.[25]

## Spain Rocked by Anti-Jewish Violence

In 1391 this distress by Spanish Christians finally boiled over. Urged on by Catholic clergymen, mobs in Seville, a major city in Castile, went on a rampage, burning synagogues, looting Jewish homes, rap-

ing Jewish women, and killing Jewish leaders. The unrest quickly spread to Cordova and other Castilian towns. Then in August of that year, the anti-Jewish riots

*Dominican monks, like this one, began preaching in Jewish ghettos throughout Spain trying to convert more Jews to Christianity.*

ESPAGNOLS. DOMINICAIN XIVᵉ SIÈCLE

swept into Aragon, where Jews in Barcelona, Saragossa, Valencia, and other towns were targeted. Some 400 Jews were massacred in Barcelona and at least 250 died in Valencia.

Faced with this dire situation, some Jews fled the country. Most of these refugees settled in North Africa, France, or Portugal. Meanwhile many other Spanish Jews tried a different strategy to evade the persecution—converting to Christianity. Beginning in 1391, the year of the great anti-Jewish riots, the number of converted Jews—called *conversos*, or "New Christians"—increased each year for several decades. The exact figures for the number of conversions in this period are unknown, but scholars estimate that between 1391 and 1415, up to one hundred thousand Jews, fully half of all the Jews in Spain, became baptized.

Seeing this trend, the Spanish authorities took steps designed to aid and strengthen it. In 1412, Catherine of Castile, then acting as regent for the underage King John II, confined the Jews to ghettos. All Jewish men were obliged to grow beards, and both male and female Jews had to sew red disks onto their outer garments to identify themselves as Jews. In addition, Jews were forbidden from becoming doctors, carpenters, blacksmiths, butchers, tailors, and tax-collectors. Jews were also forced to listen to a minimum of three Christian sermons each year. At the same time, Dominicans and

# The Expulsion of the Jews

After becoming Grand Inquisitor of the Spanish Inquisition in the early 1480s, Tomás de Torquemada repeatedly recommended to King Ferdinand and Queen Isabella that all unconverted Jews in Spain should be forcibly banished. Torquemada argued their continued presence would make it harder for the *conversos* to become devoted Christians. Eventually, the monarchs agreed. And on March 30, 1492 (the same year they granted Christopher Columbus three ships for his voyage across the Atlantic), they issued an expulsion decree. All unconverted Jews were given four months to leave the country. In one of the most shameful episodes in European history, some two hundred thousand Jews either went into exile or died in the process. Thousands were charged huge fees by ship captains and then thrown overboard in the open ocean. Thousands more were massacred and cut open by eager Christians who thought they would find jewels swallowed by Jews trying to hide their valuables. In addition, thousands of Jewish homes were looted or confiscated by Christians. Today, European Jews still remember the Spanish expulsion as a terrible act of cruelty and betrayal.

# Queen Isabella

Isabella, who created the Spanish Inquisition along with her husband, King Ferdinand, was born in Castile in 1451. She was the daughter of Castile's king, John II, and the half-sister of John's son, Henry, who ascended the throne as Henry IV in 1454. In 1469, Isabella married Ferdinand, who at the time was the young heir to Aragon's throne. When Henry died in December 1474, Isabella, then just twenty-two, wasted no time in declaring herself queen of Castile. Some leading Castilians, as well as the king of Portugal, objected, but Ferdinand helped Isabella subdue all of her opponents. Not long afterward, the royal couple began implementing policies designed to unify the Spanish kingdoms into a single, culturally homogenous nation. The creation of the Inquisition and the expulsion of the Jews were among these policies. In 1492, Isabella sponsored Christopher Columbus's first voyage across the Atlantic, which opened North and South America to Spanish explorers and initiated a global Spanish empire. Before she died in 1504, she had five children with Ferdinand, including Catherine of Aragon (b. 1485), who eventually married England's King Henry VIII.

other Christian monks began preaching in the Jewish ghettos, trying to get more Jews to convert. These rules and practices were soon put into place in Aragon as well, and later in the century, King Ferdinand and Queen Isabella tightened the enforcement of anti-Jewish regulations. All of this was designed to make unconverted Jews so miserable that they would give in and become Christians.

## Why Ferdinand and Isabella Created the Inquisition

As the years went by, many Spanish Christians expressed some serious discontent with the *conversos* in the country. These feelings would find their ultimate expression in the formation of the Spanish Inquisition during the reigns of King Ferdinand and Queen Isabella. Essentially, the growing complaint against the *conversos* was that they were "false Christians." They were charged with leading a double life and thereby trying to fool both the authorities and society. "It was said that in public they conformed with their obligations as Catholics," Perez explains, "going to mass, attending services, and distinguishing themselves as little as possible from other Christians." In the privacy of their homes, however, the *conversos* supposedly "observed the rites and practices of the law of Moses and respected the Jewish Sabbath and festivals."[26]

In 1475 some leaders of the Dominican order in Spain, along with various worried public officials, presented the charges

against the *conversos* to Ferdinand and Isabella. At first these monarchs did not feel it was necessary to use violence against the converted Jews. Isabella, who had a prominent *converso* on her staff of advisors, was particularly reluctant to launch a persecution. Eventually Ferdinand became convinced that force was the only viable option and he convinced his wife to go along with him.

Ferdinand's and Isabella's main goal in going after the *conversos*, and later persecuting the remaining unconverted Jews in Spain, appears to have been to bring order and harmony to their country. Anti-Semitism, which had always existed in Spain, had become more acute and seemed to be the cause of much public unrest. The two sovereigns reasoned that if the *conversos* were forced to become "real" and devout Christians, they would be assimilated smoothly into Spanish society. At the same time, any Jews who refused to convert could be expelled from the country. These

*After contacting Pope Sixtus IV, Ferdinand and Isabella were happy when Sixtus issued a decree authorizing the establishment of the Spanish Inquisition.*

moves would, it was hoped, reduce the incidence of anti-Semitism in society and thereby restore public order and make Spain more united and strong. In addition, Ferdinand had a lesser but still significant motive for going after the Jews, namely a financial one. An influential 19th-century Spanish writer named Juan Antonio Llorent charged:

> The extirpation [eradication] of Judaism [in Spain] was not the real cause, but the mere pretext for the establishment of the Inquisition of King Ferdinand. The true motive was to carry on a vigorous system of confiscation against the Jews, and to bring their riches into the hands of the government.[27]

## The Inquisition Formally Established

Whatever the combination of motives driving the Spanish monarchs to eliminate Judaism from Spain, they concluded that their efforts would be more effective if they had the authority and blessing of the Catholic Church. So in 1478, they contacted Pope Sixtus IV and petitioned him to approve their impending inquisition. Ferdinand and Isabella were pleased when, on November 1 of that year, Sixtus issued a decree authorizing the establishment of the Spanish Inquisition.

In an unusual move, the pope granted the right to appoint and dismiss the inquisitors to Ferdinand and Isabella, not to the Dominicans or bishops, as was the normal procedure. The first inquisitors, Juan de San Martin and Miguel de Morillo, formally began operations in Seville in September 1480. They were soon joined by several advisors from the Spanish royal court. Ferdinand made it perfectly clear to the inquisitors what was expected of them and bluntly reminded them who was in charge, saying: "Although you and the others enjoy the title of inquisitor, it is I and the queen who have appointed you, and without our support you can do very little."[28] The inquisitors responded to these words by doing a great deal. In the months that followed, hundreds of *conversos* were arrested and put on trial. Many of them received harsh sentences and some were burned at the stake, perhaps to set an example to other converted Jews suspected of only pretending to be Christians.

At first, there was a backlash against the inquisitors' methods and the harshness of the sentences they handed out. Some high-placed Spaniards, including many bishops, felt that it was inhumane to execute or otherwise punish *conversos* before at least giving them a chance to show that they could become devoted Christians. These critics complained to the pope, who expressed serious concerns about the way the new Inquisition was operating. On April 18, 1482, Sixtus issued a statement making it clear that he felt the Spanish inquisitors were doing their jobs with too much zeal:

> Many true and faithful Christians, on the testimony of [various sources]

have without any legitimate proof been thrust into secular prisons, tortured, and condemned . . . deprived of their goods and property, and handed over to the secular arm to be executed, to the peril of souls, setting a pernicious [bad] example and causing disgust to many.[29]

As might be expected, Ferdinand was none too happy about the pope's statement, feeling that the pontiff was meddling in Spain's internal affairs. On May 13, 1482, therefore, less than a month after Sixtus had issued his remarks, Ferdinand wrote to him, saying:

Things have been told to me, Holy Father, which, if true, would seem to merit the greatest astonishment. It is said that Your Holiness has granted [some of the suspected heretics] a general pardon for all the errors and crimes they have committed. . . . To these rumors, however, we have given no credence. . . . [You] have a duty to the Inquisition. . . . Take care, therefore, not to let the matter go further . . . and entrust us with the care of this question.[30]

A stronger pope may well have told Ferdinand that he was being impudent and continued to oppose the Spanish Inquisition. Sixtus evidently did not think getting into a protracted dispute with Ferdinand and Isabella was worth the time and effort. In October 1482, the pope gave in and

*Tomás de Torquemada, the "Grand Inquisitor," became the historical model of a cruel and fanatical inquisitor.*

removed his former objections to the manner in which the new Inquisition was operating.

Moreover, after Sixtus died in August 1484, his successor, Pope Innocent VIII, took the same meek stance. By this time the Inquisition's leading figure, or "Grand Inquisitor," was a monk named Tomás de Torquemada, who over time became the historical model of a cruel, fanatical inquisitor. In his appeasement of the Spanish sovereigns, Innocent went so far as to grant Torquemada the right to deal with all appeals lodged by those sentenced by the Inquisition; this was an enormous concession by the Church because in the earlier medieval Inquisition appeals were handled by the archbishop of Seville. In this situation, Torquemada, his inquisitors, and their royal patron, Ferdinand, had a free hand to run the Inquisition virtually any way they desired. This was an ominous development. Without any substantial oversight from Rome, the way was open for the Inquisition in Spain to act in a terrible and cruel manner, which in the judgment of posterity it sometimes did.

# Chapter Four

# The Spanish Inquisition: Methods and Punishments

In general, the procedures and penalties employed by those who ran the Spanish Inquisition were similar to those used in the earlier medieval Inquisition. Suspects were identified, arrested, tried, often tortured, then sentenced and punished. Some variations of these steps—as well as some new rules, methods, and tortures—came to be employed in Spain, making the Spanish Inquisition distinct from other such tribunals in medieval and early modern Europe.

Another factor that made the Inquisition in Spain unique or peculiar to its particular time and place was the attitude of the Spanish inquisitors. In the medieval Inquisition, most, if not all, of the inquisitors were convinced that they were saving the souls of the heretics they arrested and punished. They also believed that they were maintaining the integrity of the Church. In the Spanish Inquisition, by contrast, there was less concern with strictly religious goals,

including saving souls and protecting the Church in Rome. Perhaps because of the political roots and goals of the Inquisition in Spain, and the fact that it was overseen locally by secular authorities, more emphasis was placed on transforming society. The Spanish inquisitors felt they were, quite justifiably, ridding society, of unwholesome, dangerous elements and that the country would be purer and stronger when those elements were removed or brought under control. One of these inquisitors aptly summed up this goal in 1578, saying: "We must remember that the main purpose of the trial and execution [of an accused heretic] is not to save the soul of the accused, but to achieve the public good and put fear into others."[31]

Another factor that made the Spanish Inquisition different than other European inquisitions was the manner in which it was organized. In the medieval Inquisition, the popes and bishops

*The Spanish Inquisition was different than other inquisitions. One difference was the appointment of a Grand Inquisitor who oversaw all of the day-to-day operations.*

had appointed the inquisitors and had acted as their advisors and consultants, as well as final judges in religious and legal matters. In Spain, however, the king appointed the Grand Inquisitor, a choice the pope then dutifully approved by giving his blessing. The Grand Inquisitor oversaw all the day-to-day operations of the Spanish Inquisition; he was the ultimate judge and arbiter in all cases, making him a very powerful person in Spanish society. However, the Grand Inquisitor was still required to consider the advice and follow some of the directives of a special council—the *Consejo de la Suprema y General Inquisition*, often called the *Suprema* for short. The members of the *Suprema* were usually secular,

political figures appointed by the king. Once the Inquisition became entrenched in Spain, the Grand Inquisitor and the members of the *Suprema* were the most powerful and feared individuals in the country besides the king (or in the case of Isabella in Castile, the queen).

## Bringing Heretics to Trial

These individuals were able to maintain a state of fear for more than three centuries because the procedures they employed were highly organized, extremely efficient, and often brutal and inhumane. As in the earlier medieval Inquisition, the first procedure involved targeting a specific town. The local inhabitants were ordered to attend a public meeting in which an inquisitor issued an Edict of Faith, demanding that heretics confess their sins and that they and other citizens turn in suspected heretics. "The obligation to denounce all those whom one suspected of being heretics extended to all the faithful," Joseph Perez points out, "on pain of excommunication."[32] In this way, the threat of an ecclesiastical punishment—throwing someone out of the Church—was used to achieve what was essentially a political goal—to purge Jews, Muslims, Protestants, or other undesirables from society.

The Edict of Faith also supplied the potential informants in the town with the tools they needed to root out suspected heretics. For example, in the case of Spain's false Christians, that is, Jews thought to be only pretending to be Christians, the edict listed the various words and practices that were supposedly indications of a false Christian. One typical Edict of Faith issued in the 1500s in a number of Spanish towns went as follows:

If you know or have heard of anyone who keeps the Sabbath according to the law of Moses, putting on clean sheets and other new garments . . . in feast-days in honor of the Sabbath, and using no lights from Friday evening onwards; or is they have purified the meat they are to eat by bleeding it in water . . . or have eaten meat in Lent and on other days forbidden by Holy Mother Church; or have fasted the great fast, going barefooted that day; or if they say Jewish prayers at night . . . without making the sign of the cross . . . or

# Exporting the Spanish Inquisition

The Spanish Inquisition operated not only in Spain, but also in those lands that Spain came to control in the late medieval era and early modern one. For example, between 1580 and 1640, the Spanish government controlled neighboring Portugal, and branches of the Inquisition opened in Lisbon and other Portuguese cities and towns. When this happened, many of the descendants of the Jews who had fled Spain and settled in Portugal in 1492 found themselves persecuted by inquisitors trying to force them to convert to Catholicism. The Spanish Inquisition also opened branches in the so-called New World, in colonies founded by the Spanish in North and South America. In addition to heretics, inquisitors in the Americas persecuted Spaniards and others who cohabited with Native Americans, who were viewed as inferior to Europeans.

if they circumcise their children or give them Jewish names; or if after baptism they wash the place where the oil and chrism was put; or if anyone on his deathbed turns to the wall to die.[33]

One drawback of the process was that, whether the suspects were Jews, Christians, or others, not all the denunciations made by citizens against their neighbors had to do with religious faith. Frequently the informants targeted their social enemies or rivals or people who were just non-conformists. In the words of one twentieth-century Spanish observer:

People could not bear to see anyone distinguishing himself, not thinking as others did, standing out from the herd. They could not tolerate . . . personal opinions [or] thinking for oneself. . . . One had to stick to orthodoxy, the central dogma, the general opinion—or rather non-opinion [and] non-thought.[34]

This meant that the inquisitors had their work cut out for them in sifting through the many accusations of wrongdoing they received in the days and weeks following the Edict of Faith. Their initial job was to try to separate potential heretics from people who were simply odd-balls who had been denounced for being different than the norm. On occasion, when the inquisitors were unsure about how to proceed with an individual, they might ask

*Suspected heretics are brought to trial before the Spanish Inquisition after being accused by fellow citizens.*

for the advice of the *Suprema*. Eventually, the inquisitors built up files for various suspects. Each file contained "evidence" against these individuals in the form of testimony from neighbors and other local witnesses.

When the time seemed right, the inquisitors had the most likely suspects arrested and thrown in jail. Coinciding with the arrest, or *clamorosa*, the authorities seized some or all of the prisoners' property to help pay for their upkeep while confined. Well-to-do persons were allowed to bring one or two servants along with them into the Inquisition's prisons; these servants, who prepared food and performed other services for the detainees, were stuck in the jail cells for as long as their masters remained in them. The prisoners were not allowed to write letters to or to communicate in other ways with outsiders. And they were forbidden to take Holy Communion or otherwise engage in regular worship (because they were assumed to be guilty of heresy against God).

## The Trial's Initial Stages

The length of time that an accused heretic spent in jail awaiting his or her trial varied widely. Sometimes it was only a few days or weeks; other times it was months or in rare cases more than a year. Eventually, when the Grand Inquisitor deemed that it was time for the trial to begin, he ordered armed guards to bring the accused person before a panel of judges. All of these judges were inquisitors who worked for the Grand Inquisitor. Another inquisitor acted as the prosecutor.

When the suspected heretic first faced the judges, one of them read aloud the charges against him or her. Then the judges proceeded to question the person. Among other things, they asked what he or she did for a living; the names of parents, grandparents, spouses, children and other relatives; the names of friends; and all the places where the person had lived or traveled to. The accused was also required to recite standard Catholic prayers and Bible facts to establish that he or she was or had been a Christian.

Next, the inquisitors tried to get the accused to confess to the crime of heresy. (That was usually the only charge; however, if the person was guilty of other crimes, he or she was expected to confess to those, too.) Over a period of several days, the judges formally demanded a confession three times (unless the person confessed after the first time). The accused was presumed guilty unless he or she could prove otherwise. If the person refused to confess, the court appointed a lawyer to represent him or her. However, the lawyer's job was not to defend the accused, as happens in modern legal proceedings, but rather to persuade him or her to confess freely to having committed heresy. Finally, if the prisoner still refused to confess, the prosecutor brought in witnesses to prove that he or she was indeed guilty of the charges. During this phase of the trial, the accused was allowed to produce witnesses of his

*An accused heretic is questioned by inquisitors. If he doesn't confess his heresy, he will be tortured until he does.*

or her own, either to refute the prosecution's witnesses or to testify that the prisoner was an honest, moral person.

## Rationales and Rules for Torture

The major emphasis placed on getting the accused to confess stemmed from the reality that, according to its own rules, the Inquisition could not convict or punish a person without a confession. The chief judge had to proclaim, *"Habemus confitentum reum"* ("We have a confessed criminal") before sentence could be passed. The problem was that most of the people arrested by the Inquisition did not think themselves to be heretics, and a large proportion of them were unwilling to admit to that charge. That meant that in many

cases the inquisitors had to resort to some means to force the prisoners to confess. Because torture was already an accepted practice in the secular courts, it seemed only natural to use it in the inquisitional courts when forced confessions were required.

Over time, the Spanish Inquisition evolved various rules relating to the application of torture. First, the inquisitors realized that torturing someone did not always make him or her tell the truth. As Nicolas Eymerich, an inquisitor for the earlier medieval Inquisition, had written:

> Torture itself is not a certain means of discovering the truth. There are weak men, who, at the slightest pain, confess even to crimes that they did not commit, and others, stronger and more stubborn, who will bear the greatest torments.[35]

For this reason, it was not enough simply to accept the victim's confessions during torture. The accused was obliged to confirm his or her confession on the day following the torture, based on the notion that this time the admission was given freely, without coercion.

In such cases, the inquisitors conveniently ignored the fact that the prisoner

# Detailed Records Kept of Torture

*The courts of the Spanish Inquisition kept meticulous records of nearly everything they did, including what happened in the torture sessions they held. Practically every word spoken (or paraphrases of them) in these sessions was written down by a clerk. Typical is this small portion of a session in which a Belgian merchant was tortured by the inquisitors because they did not believe him when he professed to be Catholic:*

They [the inquisitors] ordered him to be given three turns of the cord [on the rack] and when these were given he was warned [to confess], and he said he had nothing to say. Then they ordered another three turns of the cord, and he was warned and said that it was true he was a Catholic and had always been and that if it were otherwise, he would say so. He was admonished to tell the truth. He said he knew no more, and if he did he would say so. When he made this reply, they ordered another three turns of the cord, and when these were given, he was admonished [once again to tell the truth].

Quoted in Walter de Gray Birch, *Catalogue of a Collection of Original Manuscripts of the Inquisition of the Canary Islands.* 2 vols. London: Somerset, 1903, vol. 1, p. 378.

was likely confessing out of fear of being tortured again. According to the rules of the Spanish Inquisition, a person could be tortured only once during his or her trial. However, everyone was aware that the inquisitors routinely circumvented this rule by calling the end of each torture session a "suspension." Thus, as Baigent and Leigh explain:

It could be claimed that a victim was indeed tortured only once, even if that "single" instance of torture included a multitude of sessions and suspensions extended over a considerable period of time. And,

of course, the victim was deprived of the hope that the end of any given session marked the end of his ordeal.[36]

Some of the other rules relating to the use of torture stipulated that it was inappropriate for the inquisitors themselves to shed blood. One way to keep them from dirtying their hands, so to speak, was to pay the local town executioner to apply the torture. Typically these outside torturers were paid by the session. They usually wore masks or hoods so that no one would recognize them, since the nature of their work made them extremely unpopular among the locals and potential targets of reprisals.

## Common Tortures

Because of the rule forbidding the shedding of blood during torture sessions, the inquisitors came to rely on certain methods that usually did not cause bleeding. Three such bloodless methods became very common in Spain. One, the *toca*,

*A prisoner is tortured using the pulley method, one of three common forms of torture used during the Spanish Inquisition.*

or water torture, involved forcing water down the victim's throat, forcing him or her to gag and creating the sensation of drowning. The person was tied to a board or ladder, which was tilted so that the victim's head was slightly lower than his or her feet. Sometimes a funnel was placed in the person's mouth and water poured into the funnel. Other times the torturer placed a cloth over the victim's mouth and kept wetting the cloth, which dripped water down the person's throat.

Also common was the *potro,* or rack torture. A rack was a large piece of wood with a wooden roller at each end. The torturers tied or chained the victim's arms and legs to the rollers and then forcefully turned the rollers, thereby stretching the victim until his or her joints throbbed with pain. There were variations of the *potro,* including some in which the ropes or chains pulled the limbs into unnatural positions. One such variation was described by William Lithgow, an English traveler captured by the Spanish in 1620 and subsequently tortured by the Inquisition. After surviving his ordeal and making it back to England, he wrote:

> The executioner . . . brought [me] to the rack and then mounted [me] on top of it. . . . The tormentor descended below, and drawing down my legs through the two sides of the three-planked rack, he tied a cord about each of my ankles and then, ascending upon the rack, he drew the cords upward, and bending forward with main [great] force my two knees against the two planks, the sinews

# Public Humiliation

*The Spanish Inquisition regularly sponsored large-scale public ceremonies known as* auto-da-fé, *in which people who had been convicted by the Inquisition were punished. This is part of a surviving contemporary description of an* auto-da-fé *held in February 1486 in the Spanish city of Toledo, in which the prisoners suffered public humiliation rather than death:*

All the [prisoners] went in procession, to the number of 750 persons, including both men and women. . . . The men were all together in a group, bareheaded and [barefoot]. . . . In their hands were unlit candles. The women were together in a group, their heads uncovered and their faces bare, unshod like the men and with candles. . . . With the bitter cold and the dishonor and disgrace they suffered from the great number of spectators . . . they went along, howling loudly and weeping and tearing out their hair. . . . At the door of the church were two chaplains who made the sign of the cross on each one's forehead. . . . Then they went into the church until they arrived at a scaffolding erected . . . and on it were the father inquisitors. . . . [As punishments, the prisoners were ordered to whip themselves] . . . and they were to fast for six Fridays. It was also ordered that all the days of their life they were to hold no public office . . . and they were ordered that if they relapsed, that is if they fell into the same error again . . . they would be condemned to the fire.

Quoted in Henry Kamen, *The Spanish Inquisition.* London: White Lion, 1976, pp. 190–191.

of my hams [i.e., hamstrings] burst asunder, and the lids of my knees [were] crushed.[37]

A third common torture employed by the Spanish Inquisition was the *garrucha*, or pulley torture, called the *strappado* in Italy and some other parts of Europe. The prisoner's feet were bound together and the hands were tied behind the back. The wrists were then attached to a rope that was itself connected to a pulley near the chamber's ceiling. Using this pulley sys-

tem, the torturers raised the victim off the floor, causing severe pain to the wrists, arms, shoulders, and chest. One variation was to suddenly drop the prisoner to the floor, often resulting in dislocation of the ankles or knees.

In the later centuries of its existence, the Spanish Inquisition instituted other tortures even more gruesome than those just described. Whatever the nature of the torture implemented, it was not unusual for the victim to be permanently maimed or disabled. Also, in some cases

*An* auto-da-fé *where nine victims are already being burned at the stake and others are being carried on horseback to meet the same fate.*

the victims died during torture sessions. When this happened, the death was pronounced an unavoidable side effect of the torture; it was also seen as the victim's own fault, since if he or she had confessed in the first place, the inquisitors would not have been "forced" to apply torture.

## Verdicts and Punishments

Those prisoners who survived the torture sessions (along with those who confessed beforehand and thereby avoided torture) faced the verdict of the inquisitional court, followed by sentencing and punishment. Acquittals were very rare and usually happened only in cases in which

it was proven that the witnesses who had accused the person had lied. Most people tried by the Inquisition throughout its long tenure in Spain were found guilty and received some form of punishment.

The penalties meted out varied widely, depending on the circumstances. Prisoners who confessed early on and were deemed to be sufficiently repentant received fairly light punishments. Among others, these included having to wear a big yellow cross (the *sanbenito*) on one's outer garments to mark him or her as a sinner; having to recite lengthy prayers several times a day, sometimes for the rest of one's life; having to go on a religious pilgrimage to a holy Christian site and return with proof of the visit; and confiscation of part of the person's property.

Those prisoners who refused to confess, as well as those who were arrested and tried by the Inquisition more than once, suffered progressively more severe punishments. These included public whippings, confiscation of all the person's property, prison sentences of various lengths, and death. In cases of the latter, the most common method was burning at the stake. This often took place at a large public ceremony known as an *auto-da-fé* ("act of faith"), in which hundreds or thousands of people gathered to watch burnings, whippings, and other punishments meted out by the Inquisition. The *autos* both demonstrated the great power wielded by the Inquisition in Spain and instilled fear in the populace. As Henry Kamen puts it, "We must take seriously the psychological impact of the atmosphere of an *auto*," and of the mere existence of the Inquisition as a pervasive institution in Spain. Many non-Catholics, Kamen points out, "were converted" to Catholicism "simply out of fear of being burnt alive."[38]

# Chapter Five

# The Many Targets of the Spanish Inquisition

The Spanish Inquisition had originally been created to deal with certain problems involving the *conversos*, Jews who had converted to Christianity. There had been a desire on the part of the monarchy to unify Spain not only politically, but also culturally and religiously. This entailed making sure that everyone, or at least the vast majority of people, in the country were Catholics. But were all of the *conversos* true Catholics? Clearly some were what the Spanish called *marranos*, meaning Jews who claimed to have converted but who still practiced Jewish rituals in secret. Supposedly for the good of the country, the Inquisition sought to root these people out. Many were tried and as many as two thousand of them were executed between 1450 and 1500 alone.

Meanwhile, in 1492 the Spanish monarchs attempted to speed up the conversion process by issuing a decree that called for the expulsion of all unconverted Jews from the country. King Ferdinand and Queen Isabella had become convinced that most Jews would prefer to convert than to leave, but they were wrong. Most of the unconverted Jews chose to go into exile. Many of those who did opt for conversion at this time became *marranos* and remained Jews within the privacy of their homes. For many years to come, indeed for at least two more centuries, a considerable proportion of the Inquisition's energies were expended in rooting out and eliminating secret Jews.

Yet this was only one aspect of the Inquisition's activities during these centuries. The inquisitors also went after other non-Catholics. Indeed, at one time or another the Spanish Inquisition targeted any and all groups and individuals who exhibited even small deviations from accepted Catholic beliefs and practices. These included both Muslims and those Muslims who had converted to Christianity, as well as various kinds of Protestants, and even Catholics who dared to worship in what appeared to be unorthodox ways.

## The Problem of Muslims in Spain

Of these various non-Catholics targeted by the Inquisition, the first to be singled out after the Jews and *conversos* were Spain's Muslims. In the earliest medieval centuries, Spain had been predominately Catholic. In the opening years of the 8th century, armies of North African Muslims, often called Moors, swept into the Iberian Peninsula and seized most of its lands. Over the next several centuries, Muslims, Christians, and Jews coexisted in the region with a minimal amount of friction (excluding periodic persecutions of Jews, then a common occurrence across Europe).

Over time, however, Christian enclaves in Spain launched campaigns to regain control. In 1212, most Muslims, whom Spanish Christians called *mudéjars*, were driven from central Spain into Granada, then a region covering much of the southern part of the peninsula. The last major refuge of Muslims in Spain, the kingdom of Granada persisted and for a while prospered, but in the centuries that followed, Castile and the other Christian kingdoms whittled away at it, steadily reducing its size. Finally, in 1492 King Ferdinand and Queen Isabella conquered Granada.

Because these Spanish monarchs dreamed of a Spain that was united both politically and culturally, the existence of large numbers of Muslims in the south presented something of a problem. Granada had long existed outside of the Spanish mainstream, so its inhabitants

## The Question of Tainted Blood

The Spanish Inquisition not only questioned the religious views of its victims, but in some cases also employed its own version of racial bigotry. First, the Inquisition decided that both Jews and Muslims belonged to a different and inferior race from Catholic Spaniards. Then the inquisitors, backed by Spanish public officials, forbade those of "bad blood" from serving as public or religious officials. Moreover, all of the descendants of Jews and Muslims were discriminated against in the same manner for generations to come. Checking people's backgrounds and bloodlines to root out Jews continued in Spain until the mid–1800s. And even after the government abolished the practice in that century, anti-Jewish prejudice and fear of marrying someone with Jewish ancestry remained strong in Spanish society.

did not seem to pose much of a threat, and at first the government's policy was to allow the *mudéjars* to practice Islam as they pleased. It was assumed that most of them would end up converting to Christianity over time.

It did not take long, however, for the more religiously conservative elements in Spain's government to grow impatient with this process, and in 1502 a new policy was announced. All *mudéjars* were ordered to convert to Christianity, and thereafter Spaniards who converted from Islam to Christianity were known as *moriscos*. But had all of the *moriscos* truly converted, or were some of them still practicing Islam in secret? The common wisdom was that many *moriscos* were retaining their old beliefs and rituals in private, and the government naturally

did not persecute and prosecute *moriscos* with the same intensity that it did Jewish *conversos.* The exact reasons for this policy are uncertain. It may have stemmed partly from the fact that Spanish Christians did not dislike Muslims with the intensity they did Jews. Muslims were seen more as political and economic rivals who happened to have different beliefs; whereas Jews were viewed as Christ-killers and degenerates who posed a direct threat to Christian orthodoxy. Also, it appears that Ferdinand, Isabella, and their immediate successors felt that time would take care of the problem of the *moriscos.* Surely, the reasoning went, their children and grandchildren would grow up as Christians and the old Islamic beliefs would steadily die out.

For these reasons, and perhaps for others, these monarchs ordered the inquisitors to show restraint in dealing with the *moriscos.* This lenient policy is indeed reflected in the relatively low number of executions of *moriscos* by the Inquisition in the 1500s. Between 1550 and 1580, only fourteen *moriscos* were found guilty of heresy by the Inquisition and burned at the stake. And in Valencia between 1530 and 1609, although some five thousand *moriscos* were charged with heresy, only a handful were executed; most suffered only confiscation of their property.

At the same time, however, rich Christian Spanish nobles saw the crackdown on the *moriscos* as an opportunity to eliminate some economic competitors. Here again, the Inquisition could be a potent

turned to the Inquisition to deal with this problem. Just as they had come to police and persecute converted Jews, the inquisitors now began to watch for *moriscos* who might be trying to fool society and the authorities.

## Dealing with the *Moriscos*

In retrospect, it is noteworthy that for a number of years the Spanish Inquisition

# Telltale Signs of Secret Muslims

*When the Spanish Inquisition entered a town and delivered an Edict of Faith, it usually alerted the citizenry to certain signs by which to identify heretics. Regarding* moriscos *(converted Muslims) who might still be practicing Islam in secret, scholar Joseph Perez summarizes the signs an edict gave to identify them:*

The edict sighted the customs of celebrating particular days and particular festivals, of fasting during [the Muslim holy days of] Ramadan, of slaughtering animals in a particular way, of performing ritual ablutions (washing arms, hands, the face, the mouth, the nose ears, legs, and private parts), and abstaining from the consumption of wine and pork . . . washing the dead, enveloping them in a clean shroud, burying them lying on their side, [and] placing a stone close to the head, along with honey, milk and other food for the soul of the deceased.

Joseph Perez, *The Spanish Inquisition*. Trans. Janet Lloyd. New Haven: Yale University Press, 2005, p. 138.

tool. As an instrument of the Spanish monarchy, the Inquisition could be used to reduce the political, social, and economic influence of the *moriscos*, even if it did not imprison or execute large numbers of them. To facilitate this approach, it would be claimed that the *moriscos*, like the Jews, supposedly belonged to a separate (and obviously inferior) race from that of the local Christians. As Henry Kamen explains:

Of the many burdens imposed on them [the Moriscos] was the racialist cult of *limpieza de sangre*, or purity of blood, by which descendants of Muslims and Jews were forbidden to hold any public office, secular or ecclesiastical, in the kingdom. . . . In 1552 the Inquisition decided that no descendants of the two races could be appointed as familiars [secular servants working in churches and monasteries]. It had already been a rule that [converted Jews] were not allowed into the priesthood. In 1573 [this rule was] extended to cover Moriscos. Shut off this way from public office . . . the Moriscos became relegated to the rank of second-class citizens, condemned to live permanently on the outer fringes of Spanish society.[39]

Eventually, even this degree of exclusion of *moriscos* was not enough to satisfy those high-ranking Spanish who viewed them as a threat. (To make that threat seem even worse, some Spaniards spread the rumor that the *moriscos* might help Moors from Africa invade and reconquer Spain, a charge that was in reality not credible.) Several proposed plans to deal with the *moriscos* circulated in the late 1500s. They included purging them by unleashing the Inquisition's full resources against them; castrating all males so that the "race" would soon die out; and shipping them all to Newfoundland, where they would likely die from the cold and other harsh conditions.

These plans were rejected in large part simply on logistical grounds. By around 1600, there were at least 300,000 *moriscos* in Spain. The Inquisition possessed considerable, but still limited resources, and its leaders realized that arresting, imprisoning, trying, and punishing such enormous numbers of people would be far too expensive and difficult. Mass castrations or relocations also appeared to be too formidable tasks to undertake for either the government or the Inquisition. Finally the government and leaders of the Inquisition decided that the best course was simply to force all *moriscos* to leave the country. Accordingly in 1609, King Philip III issued an expulsion decree similar to the one that had targeted the Jews in 1492. Nearly all of the *moriscos* left in the five years that followed. (Some went to North Africa; there, ironically, they met with prejudice because they were seen as Christians. Others ended up in France and Tunisia.)

## The Growing Protestant Threat

Part of the reason that the leading inquisitors were reluctant to go after the *moriscos* in a big way in the late 1500s and early 1600s was that by that time the Inquisition had its hands full trying to deal with a wide variety of perceived heretics. Until about 1524, the Spanish Inquisition had been mainly concerned with persecuting Jews and Muslims. In that year the inquisitors first realized that a potentially much larger threat

*The last of the Moriscos left Spain after King Phillip III issued an expulsion decree.*

loomed on the horizon—the specter of Protestantism.

The Protestants came on the scene rather suddenly. For some nine centuries there had been but one church in Europe—the Roman Catholic Church. But in the late 1400s and early 1500s the Church's leadership came under increasing criticism from within. Believing that the organization had become rich, worldly, and had strayed too far from basic Christian principles, some earnest clergymen demanded major reforms.

The situation came to a head in 1517. An outspoken German theology professor named Martin Luther (1483–1546) publicly issued a list of charges against the Church. He blasted the excess wealth and luxury enjoyed by the pope, the bishops, and the large bureaucracy of religious officials surrounding them. Luther wanted the pope and bishops to return to the simplicity and honesty supposedly displayed by the earliest Christian leaders and to better address the spiritual and earthly needs of ordinary members of their flocks.

The pope warned Luther to cease these protests; and when he refused he was excommunicated. In response, the brash Luther and his fast-growing army of supporters broke free of the Church and established a new branch of Christianity, which became known as Lutheranism. By the mid–1520s, Lutheranism, the first Protestant group, was well established in many parts of Europe, while other

*Opposite: Martin Luther was the founder of the first Protestant religion, Lutheranism.*

Protestant groups were in the midst of forming. At least at first, basic Protestant beliefs were no different than traditional Catholic ones. What initially differentiated the Protestants was their refusal to acknowledge the central authority of the pope, and their institution of reforms to correct the kinds of abuses Martin Luther had protested.

## The Inquisition vs. the Lutherans

For the most part, there was not a lot the Catholic Church could do about the Lutherans and other Protestants. The pope could not send his own papal inquisitors to root out and punish Protestants because there were simply too many of these dissenters all across Europe. The situation was different in Spain, however. The country had only about seven or eight million people in total, the vast majority of whom were still staunch Catholics. The Spanish Inquisition was already well entrenched and quite adept at rooting out and dealing with heretics and nonconformists. For the Spanish monarchs and their inquisitors, therefore, the goal became to keep Protestantism from gaining a strong foothold in the country.

To accomplish that goal, the minions of the Inquisition sought to keep the bulk of the Spanish population insulated from outside Protestant influences. Initially, they worried mainly about Lutheran influences, since the Lutherans were the first and for a while the most vocal of the Protestant sects. One source of "contamination" was Lutheran books and pamphlets being smuggled into Spain.

It came to the attention of the inquisitors that Spanish *conversos* now living in the Netherlands were translating Lutheran writings into Spanish and secretly shipping them into Spain. In 1524, the Inquisition arrested a German merchant who had brought some Lutheran literature to Valencia. In that same year, a foreign merchant ship was caught with two barrels filled with Lutheran books; agents of the Inquisition and local authorities promptly burned the volumes on the nearest beach and arrested the ship's captain. So paranoid were the inquisitors about the threat of Lutheran ideas that even a monk who had bought a Lutheran book and burned it was arrested because he had thumbed through it before destroying it.

In the eyes of the inquisitors, of course, even worse than reading Lutheran literature was actual conversion to Lutheranism. At first it was mainly foreign merchants and other outsiders who were arrested for being Lutherans. Joseph Perez describes one celebrated incident that occurred in San Sebastian in 1539:

> [Several] English traders and traders were denounced to the . . . Inquisition for making suspect [remarks] in the course of a brawl in the harbor. A Spaniard had apparently said that all English were Lutherans and the English had retorted that their country's religion was better than that practiced in Spain. You did not have to fast in order to win salvation, nor did you have to confess your sins to any man . . . but only to God. Six of these Englishmen were put on trial for Lutheranism. Some were sentenced to pay small fines or to recant publicly. Only

*Although Miguel Servet escaped capture from the Spanish Inquisition, he was later convicted of heresy by Calvinists in Geneva, Switzerland, and burned at the stake.*

one received a prison sentence. He managed to escape, was recaptured . . . [and] was burned at the stake.[40]

As time went on, however, some Spaniards, too, began to be arrested for adhering to Lutheranism. In 1542 the Inquisition arrested, convicted, and executed a Spanish businessman named Francisco de San Roman, who had converted to Lutheranism after he had been exposed to that faith on a trip to Holland. Another Spaniard who became a Lutheran, Miguel Servet, actually published a book in which he rejected many Catholic ideas. Servet was smart enough to leave the country before the agents of the Inquisition could find and arrest him. In an ironic twist, however, he also angered members of another emerging Protestant sect, Calvinism; and in 1553 some Calvinists burned him at the stake in Geneva, Switzerland!

The biggest concentrations of Lutherans in Spain were discovered in 1558 in two of Spain's chief cities, Valladolid and Seville. Among those arrested were monks, nuns, and several nobles. The number of accused Lutherans was so high that the local prisons could not hold them all; nor were there enough local inquisitors to conduct all the trials, so extra inquisitors were brought in from other cities. In large *autos-de-fé* held

in 1559 and 1560, more than fifty people were burned at the stake for embracing Lutheranism. Hundreds more received prison sentences. It is noteworthy that these persecutions horrified Lutherans and other Protestants in other parts of Europe, and they inspired the first of many Protestant denunciations of the Spanish Inquisition that would occur over the course of more than three centuries. (No such criticisms of the Spanish Inquisition were made when that organization hunted down, executed, or exiled thousands of Jews; this reflects the degree of anti-Semitism that gripped Europe at the time.)

*A woman who might have been part of the group known as the* beatas *is being interrogated by members of the Spanish Inquisition.*

## Other Victims of the Spanish Inquisition

The inquisitors in Spain did not confine their activities to rooting out and punishing only Jews, Muslims, and Protestants. Other groups whose members seemed to veer from Catholic ideas and rituals in the slightest ways became suspects of the Inquisition as well. Among these was a group of women known as the *beatas* (meaning "pious women"). Most of them were unmarried women who felt some connection to God and decided to devote their lives to him. Though not nuns in the strict sense, the *beatas* did resemble nuns, as they lived in secluded, monastery-like homes and spent most of their time in prayer and other spiritual activities. Often people from nearby communities would visit the *beatas*, who would dispense advice or spiritual comfort.

The Inquisition did not begin persecuting *beatas* until the second half of the 16th century; and it did not arrest and charge all or even a majority of them. The precise reasons that the inquisitors singled out some of the *beatas* are somewhat unclear, but it is likely that those who were arrest-

# The Spanish Inquisition and Witches

*The Spanish Inquisition did prosecute a number of people for witchcraft, but in its first three centuries of existence only a relative handful were executed for witchcraft, especially when compared to the hundreds of thousands of supposed witches burned to death in other parts of Europe in this period. In most cases, the Spanish inquisitors took the stance that witchcraft was difficult to prove and was probably only a superstition. In 1611, Alonso de Salazar, a special deputy of the* Suprema, *interviewed or studied the confessions of nearly two thousand confessed witches, both male and female, and later concluded:*

With all the Christian attention in my power, I have not found even indications from which to infer that a single act of witchcraft has really occurred. Moreover, my experience leads to the conviction that, of those availing themselves of the Edict of Grace, three-quarters and more have accused themselves and their accomplices falsely. . . . I deduce . . . that there were neither witches nor bewitched until they were talked and written about. This impressed me recently [in a town] where those who confessed stated that the matter started there [only] after [a clergyman] came there to preach about these things.

Quoted in Henry C. Lea, *A History of the Inquisition of the Middle Ages.* 4 vols. New York: Harbor Press, 1955, vol. 4, pp. 233–234.

ed were suspected of practicing some sort of magic. It is also possible the inquisitors may have found it offensive that these women claimed to have a special relationship with God even though they were not formal members of the Catholic clergy. The number of *beatas* convicted by the Inquisition is unknown.

In addition to groups of people, the Inquisition opposed and persecuted numerous individuals who were viewed as dangerous for various reasons. Even prominent churchmen were not immune. Such was the case of Bartholome Carranza, Archbishop of Toledo, one of Spain's leading Catholics. In 1559 he was arrested on two charges. First, the inquisitors claimed, Carranza had had conversations with suspected Lutherans and not reported these sessions to the Inquisition; second, the archbishop had written a religious pamphlet that contained ideas the inquisitors felt did not follow official Catholic beliefs to the letter. Because of the high rank he held within the Church, Carranza appealed to Pope Pius IV to intervene. Pius did so. In a rare turn of events, he threatened to excommunicate the entire country of Spain if Carranza was not transferred to Rome for trial. The Spanish government reluctantly gave in and the archbishop was eventually released in Italy, one of the few people arrested by the Spanish Inquisition who managed to escape its wrath.

# Chapter Six

# The Roman Inquisition vs. Science

In the 1500s, the leaders of the Catholic Church became alarmed at the sudden growth of Lutheranism and other Protestant sects. The breakaway of these alternate Christian groups, called the Reformation, created a crisis for the Church. First it siphoned away millions of its most devoted followers across many parts of Europe; second, the upsurge of Protestant reformers and denominations seemed to threaten to bring the framework of traditional Catholicism crashing down. The popes and other Catholic leaders realized that they could not turn the clock backwards and eradicate these new rival faiths. The Protestants were simply too numerous and too entrenched.

Another specter that seemed to threaten the Catholic Church during the age of the Reformation was the rapid spread of knowledge. For centuries the Church had been the major repository of knowledge in Europe, but with the invention of the printing press in the 1450s and the spread of Protestant and scientific books and pamphlets in the century that followed, Catholic leaders no longer had primary control of ideas and their dissemination. "Knowledge, so the cliché goes, is power," Baigent and Leigh point out,

and the Church wielded power largely through the knowledge it monopolized, commanded, controlled, and made available to the lay populace only, as it were, by drip-feed. With the Reformation, this situation changed dramatically. The Reformation witnessed a veritable explosion of knowledge. It was to issue from secular sources. It was to issue from the newly established Protestant "heresies," such as Lutheranism. . . . Luther's translation of the Bible into the vernacular [language of common folk] and other translations that followed . . . [made] scripture available for the first time to the layman, who could read it for himself without the . . . filtering apparatus of the priesthood.[41]

Faced with these dilemmas, Church leaders saw that their only viable strategy was to fight back. First they must find some way to maintain the unwavering allegiance of most of the remaining Roman Catholics. They must do their best to contain the spread of ideas that might challenge established church doctrines. They hoped that such efforts would bolster the Church's authority and keep the institution from further eroding.

To these ends, in the 1540s Church leaders, led by Pope Paul III, initiated a major reorganization and redoubling of their efforts to fight heresy and maintain traditional Catholic beliefs and values. Among a number of steps they took was the creation in 1542 of a new and powerful version of the Inquisition. Often called the Roman Inquisition, its official name was the "Sacred Roman Congregation and Universal Inquisition, or Holy Office." Many came to call it the "Holy Office" for short. Its first leader, or Inquisitor-General, Cardinal Giovanni Caraffa, overhauled a large mansion in Rome and outfitted it with numerous prison cells. He also gave strict orders to his inquisitors to spare no one, even the rich, famous, and powerful, if there was even the slightest suspicion of heresy.

*Pope Paul III initiated a new and powerful version of the Inquisition called the Roman Inquisition of the "Holy Office."*

# Early Victims of the Roman Inquisition

Indeed Caraffa was ready to institute nothing less than a reign of terror, believing that the Church's plight was desperate and therefore required desperate measures. Pope Paul and his successor, Julius III, were not as zealous as Caraffa and kept him from abusing the great powers of the

*A woman is accused of heresy after taking part in a banned Waldensian service. The Roman Inquisition also went after Waldensians wherever it could find them.*

inquisitional office. But in 1555 Caraffa himself ascended the Church's throne as Pope Paul IV; and from that moment the Roman Inquisition became a force to reckon with in Europe.

One of the first major tasks the new pope delegated to his inquisitors was to censor books and other writings. This was seen as a way of controlling the distribution of ideas that might damage the Church's image and credibility. In 1559, the pope and Inquisition issued the *Index Librorum Prohibitorum* ("list of

banned books"), often called the Papal Index. Near the top of the list, not surprisingly, were Martin Luther's writings and the books and pamphlets of other Protestant authors. In addition, Jewish holy writings, including the Talmud, were banned, as well as the various non-Latin translations of the Bible.

In addition to banning books, the newly revamped Inquisition in Rome went after some of the same groups that had been targeted by the medieval and Spanish Inquisitions. In 1556, for example, twelve converted Jews suspected of retaining their traditional rituals were arrested, tried, and burned in Ancona (a town situated northeast of Rome). And the Inquisition also went after Waldensians wherever it could find them.

Persecuting these traditional groups of perceived heretics occupied relatively little of the Roman Inquisition's time and energy, however. More often than not, the Holy Office concentrated on prosecuting prominent individuals—writers, philosophers, scientists, and would-be religious reformers—whose ideas and public voices seemed to pose major threats to the Catholic Church and its flock. It was hoped that these high-profile cases would set an example and discourage others from committing heresy. Even members of the Catholic hierarchy were not immune from prosecution. In 1557, for instance, the Inquisition arrested and imprisoned a cardinal (a rank in the Church second only to that of the pope). Other prominent individuals silenced included an Italian thinker beheaded in 1567 and an Italian university professor strangled to death three years later. In 1573, the Venetian master-painter Paolo Veronese (1528–1588) was charged with heresy for including dwarves and a servant with a bloody nose in a scene depicting the Last Supper of Christ. The artist escaped serious punishment by changing the setting and name of the painting to that of a feast in the house of a Jewish merchant.

The Holy Office also tried to silence a noted Italian philosopher-writer, Tomasso Campanella (1568–1639). Campanella raised the ire of the Inquisition in several ways. First, he advocated that experience, in particular learning derived from the senses, is as important in the study of philosophy as religious faith. He also questioned certain natural principles, both philosophical and scientific in nature, accepted by the Church. For these "crimes," Campanella was arrested, tortured severely, and condemned to life in prison. He suffered in a jail cell for twenty-seven years before a later pope, Urban VIII, commuted his sentence.

## New Scientific Challenges

Although Campanella was not a scientist by trade, some of his ideas dealt with scientific principles and questioned some of the accepted scientific concepts of the day. (While in jail, Campanella went so far as to write a statement of support for the famous astronomer Galileo during the latter's own battle with the Inquisition.) Indeed, in the eyes of the Church and Inquisition, even more threatening than the appearance of new philosophical and religious ideas was the onrush of modern science.

One reason that new scientific ideas suddenly seemed so threatening was that throughout most of medieval times there had been almost no scientific progress. Fully supported by the Church, standard views of nature and the universe had conformed to those of ancient Greek scholars, especially the 4th-century B.C. Athenian Aristotle. He had advocated that Earth is a large sphere that rests at the center of the universe. (As proof, he cited the fact that falling objects everywhere always move toward the center of Earth; he was unaware that this phenomenon is caused by gravity.) Aristotle also held that the cosmos (or universe) consisted of a series of large, invisible spheres that nested within one another. A planet or other heavenly body (such as the moon or sun) moved along the surface of each sphere, he argued. During the 1300s, 1400s, and 1500s, the Catholic Church agreed with these ideas and incorporated them into its own scientific world view. The most important aspect of this view was that Earth and humanity together constituted the centerpiece of God's creation.

But some late medieval scholars came to the conclusion that this Earth-centered, or geocentric, view of the cosmos was in error. The great turning point came in 1543 when Polish astronomer Nicolas Copernicus proposed a sun-centered, or heliocentric, view. According to Copernicus in his *On the Revolutions*:

The sun is the center of the universe. Moreover, since the sun remains stationary, whatever appears as a

*A diagram of Nicolas Copernicus's sun-centered view of the universe. This was in opposition to the Church's Earth-centered view and lead to the persecution of many scientists.*

motion of the sun is really due rather to the motion of the Earth. . . . The size of the universe is so great that the distance Earth-sun is imperceptible in relation to the sphere of the fixed stars. This should be admitted, I believe, in preference to perplexing the mind with an almost infinite multitude of spheres, as must be done by those who kept the Earth in the middle of the universe.[42]

Clearly, the Church viewed these statements as both a challenge and a threat; and Copernicus's book ended up on the Holy Office's list of forbidden writings.

# The Inquisition vs. Giordano Bruno

Despite the fact that the Church frowned on Copernicus's theory, his ideas steadily gained adherents in some scholarly circles. Among the leading Copernicans of the sixteenth century was Giordano Bruno (1548–1600), an Italian monk who became a poet, philosopher, and brilliant astronomer. An outspoken, argumentative, fearless individual, Bruno did more than accept and support the idea that Earth is merely part of the sun's planetary system. He also advocated that there must be planetary systems orbiting other stars; moreover, he said, there are surely intelligent beings inhabiting the planets in those systems. In 1585, in a work titled *The Ash Wednesday Supper*, he stated:

> Our world, called the terrestrial globe, is identical as far as material composition goes with the other worlds, the [orbiting] bodies of other stars; and . . . it is childish to . . . believe otherwise. Also . . . there live and strive on them [the distant planets] many and innumerable . . . individuals to no less extent than we see these living and growing on the back of this [Earth] . . . . Once this is admitted, many secrets of nature, hitherto hidden, do unfold.[43]

*Giordano Bruno was tortured and finally executed because he would not recant his belief in Copernicus's sun-centered universe theory.*

# Proving Earth is Round

*The Roman Inquisition tried to maintain conformity of belief in the world view the Catholic Church then embraced. In large degree that view followed the ideas of the ancient Greek scholar Aristotle. In his treatise* On the Heavens, *Aristotle offered the following evidence to prove that Earth is a sphere:*

As it is, the shapes which the Moon itself each month shows are of every kind—straight, gibbous, and concave—but in eclipses the outline is always curved. And, since it is the interposition of the Earth [between the Sun and Moon] that makes the eclipse, the form of this line will be caused by the form of the Earth's surface, which is therefore spherical.

Quoted in Morris R. Cohen and I. E. Drabkin, *A Source Book in Greek Science.* Cambridge, MA: Harvard University Press, 1948, p. 148.

Such ideas were bound to attract the attention of the Inquisition. So Bruno eventually left Italy, where the reach of the inquisitors was strongest, and began lecturing and preaching in various foreign countries, including Germany, France, and England. He taught for a while in France. There he also enjoyed the protection of a number of noblemen, including King Henry III, who shielded him from the Inquisition's henchmen. During his travels, Bruno wrote some twenty books, advocating, among other things, that the universe is infinite in scope.

As long as Bruno stayed out of Italy and remained surrounded by people who admired him, the agents of the Inquisition were unable to arrest him. In 1591, however, he took a chance and returned to his native country. Almost immediately, an Italian nobleman whom he thought was his friend denounced him to the Holy Office, which ordered his arrest. Bruno was tried for heresy. And when he refused to recant his beliefs about the universe, the inquisitors began torturing him. Month after month, year after year, he suffered unbelievably cruel physical abuse, but his tormentors were never able to break him; through it all, he remained steadfast and even had the audacity to try to convert the inquisitors to Copernicus's theory. Finally, the leaders of the Holy Office decided that they had had enough of Bruno. At their order, on February 17, 1600 he was burned at the stake in Rome. They also ordered that the scientist be gagged while on his way to the scaffold to keep him from contaminating the spectators with his heresies.

*Using the telescope he constructed, Galileo found proof that the Earth rotated around the sun. He thought that this proof would convince Church authorities that Copernicus had been correct.*

## Galileo and the Telescope

Bruno's persecution and execution demonstrated that it was not yet safe to advocate Copernicus's views openly, but that did not keep various perceptive scientists and other intellectuals from concluding that these views were right. Sooner or later, some prominent individual was

bound to challenge the Church again on these matters and in so doing become a martyr to the cause of modern science.

That martyr, by far the most famous opponent of the Church and Inquisition in this period, turned out to be a younger contemporary of Bruno's, the brilliant Italian scientist Galileo Galilei. Born in

# The Church Finally Admits Its Error

*In 1992, Pope John Paul II became the first leading Catholic churchman to publicly admit that the Church and its inquisitors had been wrong in arresting and punishing Galileo in the 1600s. Among other things, John Paul said:*

The problem posed by theologians of that age was . . . the compatibility between heliocentrism and Scripture. Thus the new science, with its methods and the freedom of research which they implied, obliged theologians to examine their own criteria of scriptural interpretation. Most of them did not know how to do so. Paradoxically, Galileo, a sincere believer, showed himself to be more perceptive in this regard than the theologians who opposed him. . . . The majority of theologians did not recognize the formal distinction between Sacred Scripture and its interpretation, and this led them unduly to transpose into the realm of the doctrine of the faith a question which in fact pertained to scientific investigation. . . . In fact, the Bible does not concern itself with the details of the physical world, the understanding of which is the competence of human experience and reasoning.

Quoted in *L'Osservatore Romano*, November 4, 1992, pp. 3–4.

the northern Italian town of Pisa on February 15, 1564, Galileo early became a supporter of Copernicus's heliocentric theory, but the young scientist was more circumspect and cautious than Bruno. For fear of the Inquisition's wrath, Galileo long refrained from publicly endorsing the Copernican theory. Part of the reason for this strategy was that he felt there was not yet enough irrefutable evidence to convince the religious authorities that the heliocentric view was correct.

Galileo eventually came to believe that he had the evidence he needed to change the minds of Church leaders. In 1609 he heard that some Dutch spectacle makers had recently invented a device that used a system of lenses to magnify images of distant objects. It became known as the telescope. Galileo soon built his own telescope and became the first person ever to use such an instrument to study the heavens. In November 1609, he gazed through his eyepiece at the Moon and saw that its surface is covered with craters and mountain chains. A few months later Galileo discovered the four largest moons of Jupiter. He saw their movements around that planet as definitive proof that not all heavenly bodies revolve around Earth; this meant that the geocentric view of the universe was false. Surely, he thought, the fathers of the Church would believe the evidence of their own eyes.

But Galileo was wrong. Many churchmen simply refused to look through the scientist's telescope and some flatly informed him that Copernicus's ideas had to be wrong. In addition, a prominent Dominican monk, Tommaso Caccini, called science the work of the devil and said that the idea that Earth moves around the sun was heresy.

Earnestly but naively, Galileo, who was a devout Catholic, felt he had a duty to guide the Church away from such backward views and toward sound scientific principles. So he spent several years writing a book that discussed in detail the leading astronomical opinions of the day, including the heliocentric view. The book, titled *Dialogue Concerning the Two Chief World Systems,* was completed in 1629. The official Catholic censor in Rome reviewed and approved it and when it appeared in print in February 1632 it quickly sold out. These developments convinced Galileo that the Church was ready to embrace modern scientific ideas.

## Modern Science Defeated?

But once again the scientist had miscalculated. Only a few months after the book's publication the Church reversed itself and halted further printing of the book. The pope turned the matter over to the Inquisition, which ordered Galileo to stand trial for heresy. In April 1633 he was confined to the building in Rome that housed the offices of the Inquisition.

*Galileo stands trial before the Inquisition on the charge of heresy for believing that the sun is the center of the universe.*

Because he had long been friendly with the pope and a number of cardinals and bishops, he was not thrown into a dungeon, but instead occupied a comfortable suite of rooms and was allowed a servant to help him with his daily needs.

The trial consisted of four interrogation sessions, each called a deposition, in which a panel of inquisitors questioned Galileo with the intention of establishing his heresy. During these sessions, he was allowed to make statements in his own defense. Later, the inquisitors reported the outcomes of the depositions to ten cardinals who had been selected to be Galileo's judges. In what constituted the second part of the trial, they debated what sentence to give the scientist and imposed that sentence.

The Inquisition found Galileo guilty, which surprised no one. Part of the official sentence handed down by the judges read as follows:

> [We] declare that you, Galileo ... have rendered yourself ... vehemently suspect of heresy, namely of having held and believed a doctrine that is false and contrary to the divine and Holy Scripture, namely

# Galileo's Friends Within the Church

*During his imprisonment by the Inquisition, unlike many other victims of that tribunal Galileo was not physically abused, isolated, or abandoned. In fact, he lived in a comfortable apartment and enjoyed the support of a number of high-placed churchmen, including some of the inquisitors. These supporters agreed that the scientist was guilty of advocating Copernicus's heliocentric theory, but they also agreed that Galileo was a good man who did not deserve to be humiliated. One friendly churchman, Father Vincent Firenzuola, met privately with Galileo and assured him that if he admitted he had erred, it could be arranged for him to receive a light sentence—perhaps only a few months of house arrest. Firenzuola later recalled:*

I entered into discourse with Galileo ... and after many arguments ... had passed between us, by God's grace, I ... brought him to a full sense of his error, so that he clearly recognized that he had ... gone too far in his book. ... He requested, however, a little time in order to consider the form in which he might most fittingly make the confession.

Quoted in Galileo Galilei, *Le Opere di Galileo Galilei*, ed. Antonio Favaro. 20 vols. Florence, Italy: G. Barbera Editrice, 1968, vol. 15, p. 107.

that the sun is the center of the world and does not move. . . . First, with a sincere heart and unfeigned faith, in our presence you [must] abjure [renounce], curse and detest the said errors and heresies. . . . Furthermore, so that this grievous and pernicious error . . . of yours may not go altogether unpunished . . . we condemn you to formal imprisonment in this Holy Office at our pleasure.[44]

Per these orders, on June 22, 1633 the sixty-nine-year-old Galileo knelt before leading members of the Church and Inquisition and declared that he did not believe that Earth moved around the sun. "I must altogether abandon the false opinion that the sun is the center of the world and immovable," he stated.[45] Thereafter, the defeated scientist remained under house arrest until his death in January 1642.

There is no doubt that the leaders of the Roman Inquisition felt they had triumphed by forcing Galileo to recant. Surely, they reasoned, they had made an example of him and kept new ideas from challenging traditional, cherished Church doctrines, but this attitude amounted to little more than self-delusion. The reality was that modern science, far from being defeated, was just beginning to gain acceptance. Moreover, though no one could foresee it at the time, the Inquisition's own days as a powerful institution were almost over.

# The End of the Inquisition

After Galileo's prosecution for heresy by the Roman Inquisition in 1633, the remaining life of the Inquisition roughly paralleled the state of the Catholic Church's stance on the heliocentric theory. Both the Inquisition and the Church's mistaken views of the heavens remained in place for centuries to come, but they both became increasingly antiquated, less influential, and eventually had to be abandoned.

In the case of the Church's stance on the nature of the universe, by 1700 all scientists, including those who were priests, accepted the fact that Earth revolves around the Sun. Yet as late as 1819, the Papal Index still banned Copernicus's and Galileo's writings, and the Church's own astronomers dared not publish books or deliver lectures that contradicted the Church's official opinion on the subject. Fortunately, the following year one of these priest-astronomers, Canon Settele, boldly asked Pope Pius VII to modern-

ize the Church's stance. Pius referred the matter to the Holy Office, which issued the following statement in September 1822: "The printing and publication of works treating of the motion of the Earth and the stability of the sun, in accordance with the opinion of modern astronomers, is permitted at Rome."[46]

## The Inquisition in Disgrace and Decline

One is immediately struck by how much this tolerant statement made by the Inquisition in 1822 differs in content and tone from the intolerant positions taken by the Inquisition in earlier centuries. What had happened to that once stern and much feared institution to make it sound so open-minded and reasonable? The answer is that no single event caused the Inquisition to change. Rather, a long series of political, religious, and scientific events and trends made the older, more forceful Inquisition outmoded; and over time Church leaders altered its mission and methods accordingly.

One of the major factors in the decline of the old Inquisition was the onrush of enlightened political thinking and democratic revolutions in Europe. First came the European Enlightenment, which began in the late 1600s and lasted until the early 1800s. This intellectual movement, driven primarily by liberal English, French, and eventually American thinkers, celebrated human reason, newly discovered scientific facts, religious toleration, the existence of certain basic natural human rights, and fair government. Enlightenment philosophers held that science might reveal the true nature of the world, which humans could then remake, control, and exploit to their advantage. The Enlightenment's ideas steadily and profoundly changed the way educated people in Europe and elsewhere viewed certain political and social institutions that had been taken for granted for many centuries. Among these institutions were the Catholic Church and the Inquisition. Both came to be seen by Protestants and other non-Catholics, and even by some Catholics, as old-fashioned and in need of reform.

These feelings about the Inquisition were transformed into action in dramatic fashion in the late 1700s. In 1789, France was torn asunder by the French Revolution, in which radical democrats overthrew the country's monarchy. The leaders of the revolution and many ordinary French citizens now saw the Inquisition as an oppressive tool of the old regime, and they destroyed all vestiges of that institution that they could find. The same thing happened on a larger scale during the Napoleonic Wars that occurred in the following decades. As French armies swept across much of Europe, the soldiers ransacked the Inquisition's prisons, chased away or killed the inquisitors, and captured or destroyed thousands of the Inquisition's documents and records. When Napoleon's troops invaded Italy in 1798, the pope fled and the Inquisition was forced to temporarily shut down.

*Pope Pius VII was persuaded to send the matter regarding the sun-centered universe to the Holy Office, so that the Holy Office might consider changing its opinion on the subject.*

# The Congregation for the Doctrine of the Faith

After the Napoleonic Wars, the Church reinstated the Holy Office. However the Inquisition no longer wielded the power or instilled the high degree of fear that it had in the past. Clearly, it was no longer viable for the Church's agents to persecute, imprison, torture, and burn those who disagreed with traditional church doctrines. So in 1852 the Church permanently eliminated these punitive functions of the Inquisition. All prisoners then held in Inquisition jails were released and most of that institution's remaining documents were burned (to the great regret of modern historians!).

The Holy Office itself was not abolished, however. In fact, it still existed in 2007 in heavily altered form. In 1908 Pope Pius X changed its name to the Supreme Sacred Congregation of the Holy Office, and in 1965 Pope Paul VI changed it again to the Sacred Congregation for the Doctrine of the Faith. (The term *Sacred* was dropped in 1983.) In 1988, the widely popular Pope John Paul II defined the Congregation's purpose this way:

> The duty proper to the Congregation for the Doctrine of the Faith is to promote and safeguard the doctrine on the faith and morals throughout the Catholic world. For this reason, everything which in any way

*French troops enter Rome. When Napoleon's troops invaded Italy in 1798, the pope fled and the Inquisition had to shut down temporarily.*

*The Holy Office still exists as the Congregation for the Doctrine of the Faith. In 1988, Pope John Paul II defined its modern-day purpose.*

touches such matter falls within its competence.[47]

Essentially, the mission of this remnant of the once feared Inquisition is to promote and defend Catholic rules and ideas, particularly those dealing with subjects of a moral or ethical nature, such as abortion, euthanasia, and homosexuality.

## Lessons of the Inquisition

The rise and fall of the various inquisitions that spread fear and suffering throughout much of Europe for centuries left behind a legacy that still exists in Western culture. The memory of the Inquisition's cruelties remains alive in popular novels and movies, for instance. One of the most vivid examples is the 1986 film *The Name of the Rose,* based on the novel by Umberto Eco. In the story, a churchman, played by Sean Connery, clashes with the Inquisition in Italy in the year 1327. In addition, several modern plays and films have portrayed Joan of Arc's trial and execution by the Inquisition.

Also part of the Inquisition's legacy are certain lessons society has learned. First, religious faith and excess religious zeal are not one in the same. Thus, one can continue to support the Catholic Church and its doctrines even though at one time the Church allowed some of its agents to go too far in promoting those doctrines. As Baigent and Leigh put it: "It would be a mistake . . . to identify the Inquisition with the Church as a whole. They are not the same institution. [The Inquisition] remains only one aspect of the Church" and its long history.[48]

The excesses of the Inquisition in its various forms over the centuries also show that, as the old adage goes, absolute power corrupts absolutely. Church leaders gave the inquisitors authority to persecute and even kill people merely for thinking or worshiping in a certain way. This great power over people's lives was, thanks to the darker aspects of human nature, bound to be abused. The lesson learned is that no institution or government should hold such intrusive authority over people's personal lives and beliefs.

Finally, it must be observed that, despite its many persecutions and cruelties, the Inquisition failed to stop the repeated expression of individualism and new ideas. It could not break Joan of Arc's courageous spirit, nor could it halt the rise of Protestantism and modern science. This shows that the human spirit has an amazing resiliency and thirst for freedom of thought and action. Simply put, though some individuals may be silenced along the way, in the long run it is impossible to force people to believe something that they do not want to believe. The agents of the Inquisition did not understand this simple truism of the human condition, and that is why they were doomed to ultimate failure.

# Notes

## Introduction: Trying to Examine the Inquisition Impartially

1. Michael Baigent and Richard Leigh, *The Inquisition*. East Sussex, UK: Gardners, 2000, pp. xv–xvi.
2. Edward Peters, *Inquisition*. Berkeley: University of California Press, 1989, p. 57.
3. Henry Kamen, *The Spanish Inquisition*. London: White Lion, 1976, p. 284.
4. Quoted in Kamen, *Spanish Inquisition*, p. 286.
5. Ingram Cobbin, ed., *John Foxe's Book of Martyrs*. London: Knight and Son, 1856, p. 1060.
6. Quoted in *The Catholic Encyclopedia for School and Home*. 12 vols. New York: McGraw-Hill, 1965, vol. 5, p. 475.

## Chapter 1: The Medieval Inquisition: Origins and Methods

7. Quoted in Bernard Hamilton, *The Medieval Inquisition*. New York: Holmes and Meier, 1981, p. 43.
8. Anne Fremantle, *Age of Faith*. New York: Time, 1965, p. 12.
9. Louise Collis, *Memoirs of a Medieval Woman: The Life and Times of Margery Kempe*. New York: Harper and Row, 1964, p. 11.
10. Quoted in Emmanuel Le Roy Ladurie, *Montaillou*. New York: Vintage, 1975, pp. 78, 81.

11. Quoted in Jonathan Sumption, *The Albigensian Crusade*. London: Faber and Faber, 1978, p. 93.
12. Quoted in Marie-Humbert Vicaire, *St. Dominic and His Times*. New York: McGraw-Hill, 1964, p. 146.
13. Quoted in Henry C. Lea, *A History of the Inquisition of the Middle Ages*. 4 vols. New York: Harbor Press, 1955, vol. 1, p. 329.
14. Quoted in Lea, *History of the Inquisition*, vol. 1, p. 329.
15. Baigent and Leigh, *Inquisition*, p. 28.
16. Baigent and Leigh, *Inquisition*, pp. 30–31.
17. Quoted in A.L. Maycock, *The Inquisition*. London: Constable, p. 173.

## Chapter 2: Victims and Martyrs of the Medieval Inquisition

18. Quoted in Reinerius Saccho, *Of the Sects of the Modern Heretics*, (www.fordham.edu/halsall/source/waldo2.html)
19. Quoted in Lea, *History of the Inquisition*, vol. 1, p. 296.
20. Baigent and Leigh, *Inquisition*, p. 48.
21. Quoted in Régine Pernoud, Joan of Arc: By Herself and Her Witnesses. Trans. Edward Hyams. Chelsea, MI: Scarborough House, 1994, p. 184.
22. Quoted in Wilfred T. Jewkes and Jerome B. Landfield, eds., *Joan of Arc: Fact, Legend, and Literature*. New York: Harcourt, Brace and World, 1964, p. 78.

## Chapter 3: Origins and Goals of the Spanish Inquisition

23. Quoted in Rosemary Horrox, ed., *The Black Death*. Manchester, Eng.: Manchester University Press, 1994, p. 45.
24. Joseph Perez, *The Spanish Inquisition*. Trans. Janet Lloyd. New Haven: Yale University Press, 2005, pp. 4–5.
25. Perez, *Spanish Inquisition*, p. 10.
26. Perez, *Spanish Inquisition*, p. 6.
27. Quoted in Paul J. Hauben, ed., *The Spanish Inquisition*. New York: Wiley, 1969, p. 38.
28. Quoted in Baigent and Leigh, *Inquisition*, p. 63.
29. Quoted in Kamen, *Spanish Inquisition*, pp. 47–48.
30. Quoted in Kamen, *Spanish Inquisition*, p. 48.

## Chapter 4: The Spanish Inquisition: Methods and Punishments

31. Quoted in "The Inquisition and Slavery" (www.positiveatheism.org/hist/ellerbe0.htm)
32. Perez, *Spanish Inquisition*, p. 136.
33. Quoted in Kamen, *Spanish Inquisition*, pp. 165–166.
34. Quoted in Perez, *Spanish Inquisition*, p. 141.
35. Quoted in Perez, *Spanish Inquisition*, p. 147.
36. Baigent and Leigh, *Inquisition*, p. 71.
37. Quoted in Edward Burman, *The Inquisition: The Hammer of Heresy*. London: Aquarius, 1984, p. 23.
38. Kamen, *Spanish Inquisition*, p. 185.

## Chapter 5: The Many Targets of the Spanish Inquisition

39. Kamen, *Spanish Inquisition*, pp. 115–116.
40. Perez, *Spanish Inquisition*, p. 62.

## Chapter 6: The Roman Inquisition vs. Science

41. Baigent and Leigh, *Inquisition*, p. 124.
42. Nicholas Copernicus, *On the Revolutions*, trans. Edward Rosen. Baltimore: Johns Hopkins University Press, 1992, p. 38.
43. Giordano Bruno, *The Ash Wednesday Supper*, trans. Stanley L. Jaki. Dartmouth College, 1999, p. 7. (http://hilbert.dartmouth.edu/~matc/Readers/renaissance.astro/6.1.Supper.html)
44. Quoted in Galileo Galilei, *Le Opere di Galileo Galilei*, ed. Antonio Favaro. 20 vols. Florence, Italy: G. Barbera Editrice, 1968, vol. 19, p. 406.
45. Quoted in Galileo, *Le Opere di Galileo Galilei*, vol. 19, p. 406.

## Epilogue: The End of the Inquisition

46. Quoted in John O'Brien, *The Inquisition*. New York: Macmillan, 1973, p. 208.
47. Quoted in "Congregation for the Doctrine of the Faith" (part of the official web site of the Catholic Church). (www.vatican.va/roman_curia/congregations/cfaith/docu ments/rc_con_cfaith_pro_14071997_en.html)
48. Baigent and Leigh, *Inquisition*, p. xv.

# For More Information

## Books

Michael Baigent and Richard Leigh, *The Inquisition*. East Sussex, UK: Gardners, 2000. Very well researched, this is one of the best modern studies of all three of the main phases of the Inquisition.

Mike Goldsmith, *Galileo Galilei*. New York: Raintree/Steck Vaughn, 2002. One of the better presentations for young readers of Galileo's contributions to science and his famous run-in with the Inquisition.

Henry Kamen, *The Spanish Inquisition: A Historical Revision*. New Haven: Yale University Press, 1999. Kamen has made an important contribution to scholarship about the Inquisition by putting the subject into perspective and pointing out exaggerations and myths associated with the Inquisition.

Jerome J. Langford, *Galileo, Science, and the Church*. Ann Arbor: University of Michigan Press, 1992. A superior study of Galileo's intellectual differences with the Church, culminating in his trial.

Joseph Perez, *The Spanish Inquisition*. Trans. Janet Lloyd. New Haven: Yale University Press, 2005. A detailed and balanced look at the operations of the Inquisition in Spain, the most infamous and controversial phase of the Inquisition.

Régine Pernoud, *Joan of Arc: By Herself and Her Witnesses*. Trans. Edward Hyams. Chelsea, MI: Scarborough House, 1994. One of the best available overviews of Joan's life, including detailed testimony from her trial by the Inquisition.

Edward Peters, *Inquisition*. Berkeley: University of California Press, 1989. One of the more controversial and often-cited books about the Inquisition, this one, like Henry Kamen's well-known tome, makes the case that some of the so-called crimes of the Inquisition have been exaggerated by later observers.

Michael White, *The Pope and the Heretic: The True Story of Giordano Bruno, the Man Who Dared to Defy the Roman Inquisition*. New York: Harper Perennial, 2003. A well-written study of one of the most fascinating thinkers of the late Middle Ages and how he lost his life to the Inquisition.

## Web Sites

Giordano Bruno, *The Ash Wednesday Supper.* Trans. Stanley L. Jaki. Dartmouth College, 1999. http://hilbert.dartmouth.edu/~matc/Readers/renaissance.astro/6.1.Supper.html One of the two major astronomical works of the Italian priest and astronomer whom the Inquisition burned at the stake.

Robert Jones, "A Brief History of the Inquisition," 1998. http://www.sundayschoolcourses.com/inq/inqcont.htm

Douglas Linder, "The Trial of Galileo," 2002. (www.law.umkc.edu/faculty/projects/ftrials/galileo/galileo.html) A useful collection of some of the main documents associated with Galileo's confrontation with the Inquisition.

# Index

# Picture Credits

© AAAC/Topham/The Image Works, 27

© Albert Harlingue/Roger-Viollet/The Image Works, 34

© Ann Ronan Picture Library/Heritage-Images/The Image Works, 8, 11, 76

Anonymous, 17th century, Portrait of William III (1650–1702) as Prince of Orange, Dutch, ca. 1670–1687. He wears the armor of Charles I and Charles II and rests his left hand on a helmet. © The Board of Trustees of the Armouries Institution. HIP / Art Resource, NY., 13

© Antman Archives/The Image Works, 67

AP Images, 9, 90

Archive Photos/Getty Images, 32

The Art Archive/Academia BB AA S Fernando Madrid, 54–55

The Art Archive/Bibliothéque Universitaire Geneva/Dagli Orti, 70

The Art Archive/Bibliotheque de Carcassonne/Dagli Orti, 17

The Art Archive/Cabildo Cathedral Burgos, 64–65

The Art Archive/Museo de Arte Antiga Lisbon/Dagli Orti, 8

The Art Archive/Museo del Prado Madrid/Dagli Orti, 26

The Art Archive/Pinacoteca Nazionale Bologna/Dagli Orti (A), 87

The Art Archive/Pinacoteca Virreinel Mexico City/Dagli Orti, 15

The Catholic University of America, 79

© Charles Walker/Topham/The Image Works, 71

The Entrance of the French Army into Rome led by Marshall Berthier, 15th February 1798, pub. by Goupil, Paris (engraving), /Private Collection, Roger-Viollet, Paris/The Bridgeman Art Library International, 88–89

Hulton Archive/Getty Images, 9, 12, 24, 41, 58, 78, 81, 83

The Jones Brothers Publishing Company, 1890, 8

The Library of Congress, 9

© Mary Evans Picture Library/The Image Works, 21, 30, 41, 46–47, 56, 60

MPI/Getty Images, 40

Ms Fr.6465 f.236 The Supplication of the Heretics in 1210 (vellum) (see also 51339), Fouquet, Jean (c. 1420–80)/Bibliotheque Nationale, Paris, France, /The Bridgeman Art Library International, 22

Or. MS 2884 f.17v A Synagogue, c. 1350, Northern Spain (Hebrew manuscript) (vellum), Spanish School, (14th century)/British Library, London, UK, /The Bridgeman Art Library International, 42

Photodisc Blue/Getty Images, 52

Roger Viollet Collection/Getty Images, 75

© Stefano Bianchetti/Corbis, 48–49

Stock Montage/Getty Images, 68

Thomson Gale, 19

Time & Life Pictures/Getty Images, 35

# About the Author

In addition to his acclaimed volumes on the ancient world, historian Don Nardo has produced several studies of medieval times, including *Life on a Medieval Pilgrimage, The Medieval Castle, The Black Death,* and *The Italian Renaissance.* He has also produced volumes about medieval warfare and the King Arthur legends. Mr. Nardo resides with his wife Christine in Massachusetts.